# Gathering Voices

D1246339

# Gathering Voices

CREATING A COMMUNITY-BASED
POETRY WORKSHOP

*Marty McConnell*

YESYES BOOKS, PORTLAND

GATHERING VOICES:

CREATING A COMMUNITY-BASED POETRY WORKSHOP

© 2018 BY MARTY MCCONNELL

COVER & INTERIOR DESIGN: ALBAN FISCHER

LEAD EDITORS: STEVIE EDWARDS AND KMA SULLIVAN

ALL RIGHTS RESERVED.

NO PART OF THIS BOOK MAY BE REPRODUCED

WITHOUT THE PUBLISHER'S WRITTEN PERMISSION,

EXCEPT FOR BRIEF QUOTATIONS FOR REVIEWS.

ISBN 978-1-936919-56-7

PRINTED IN THE UNITED STATES OF AMERICA

PUBLISHED BY YESYES BOOKS

1614 NE ALBERTA ST

PORTLAND, OR 97211

YESYESBOOKS.COM

KMA SULLIVAN, PUBLISHER

JOANN BALINGIT, ASSISTANT EDITOR

STEVIE EDWARDS, SENIOR EDITOR, BOOK DEVELOPMENT

ALBAN FISCHER, GRAPHIC DESIGNER

COLE HILDEBRAND, SENIOR EDITOR OF OPERATIONS

JILL KOLONGOWSKI, MANAGING EDITOR

BEYZA OZER, DEPUTY DIRECTOR OF SOCIAL MEDIA

AMBER RAMBHAROSE, CREATIVE DIRECTOR OF SOCIAL MEDIA

CARLY SCHWEPPE, ASSISTANT EDITOR, *VINYL*

LEVI TODD, SOCIAL MEDIA INTERN

PHILLIP B. WILLIAMS, COEDITOR IN CHIEF, *VINYL*

AMIE ZIMMERMAN, EVENTS COORDINATOR

HARI ZIYAD, ASSISTANT EDITOR, *VINYL*

# CONTENTS

# Gathering Voices

# CHAPTER ONE

# *Welcome*

Dear Reader,

Almost 20 years ago, I entered the MFA program at Sarah Lawrence College having never taken a single creative writing class. Until then, my only workshop experience was a group of smart women gathered weekly in a living room to look at each other's poems through a not terribly learned but absolutely devoted lens. I didn't know anaphora from anapest, and I didn't care.

What I did care about was poetry, and in that program I found people who wanted to talk about poetry all the time, and who could open poetry for me in deep and transformative ways.

After finishing that MFA, I worked for almost ten years to build an all-volunteer poetry organization in New York City called The louderARTS Project. In addition to running a weekly poetry series, we coordinated salons, regular writing workshops, thematic showcases, and the occasional unofficial house party.

As I witnessed, hosted, taught, listened, debated, wrote, and read, I saw how poetry can forge connections among people that transcend vast differences in their backgrounds, educational levels, cultural grounding, gender expression, etc. In open mics and slams, in salons and bar arguments, and especially in workshops, I found that poetry flourished through community, and probably more importantly, community flourished through poetry.

When I left New York and returned to my hometown of Chicago in 2009, the part of that work that felt most crucial to continue was the community-based workshopping. I joined forces with one of the women from that long-ago living room group and started offering what we called "Vox Ferus" workshops—"fierce voice" in Latin (kinda).

Since then, the workshop process has grown and evolved into what is described in this book as the Gathering Voices approach. I've continued to run these workshops about once a month out of my home, as well as the occasional library, acupuncture studio, coffee shop, and bar.

I wanted to make sure that money was not a barrier, so the workshops are by donation only, no one turned away for lack of funds. I wanted participants to connect as people as well as poets, so there is time built in for mingling, and everyone is encouraged to bring food and drink to partake of and share.

Most of all, I wanted to ensure that people with all levels of experience and education were welcomed and unintimidated. To work toward this goal, I developed a few fundamental practices for this workshop:

- *Curiosity* about new perspectives, approaches, and possibilities, as opposed to criticism and competition.
- *Receptivity* to ideas, to art, to each other.
- *Joy* in the work and in the community.
- *Rigor* in our approach to growth, both our own and other people's.

From these practices evolved a sort of code of conduct that guides how we interact within the workshop model:

- We value the potential, the experience, and the perspective each person brings. This is reflected in our words, actions, and attitudes.
- We approach poems not as broken things in need of fixing, nor as objects of like or dislike, but as subjects of study and analysis, artworks whose possibilities we get to unpack.

- We come ready to work. Eager to engage. Committed to creating a positive, challenging environment for everyone.

The Gathering Voices approach does not aim to create great poets, though certainly a solid workshop practice that includes examination of diverse and exceptional poems by established writers will almost invariably improve one's writing.

Rather, these workshop plans provide a practical, easy-to-follow way for people to come together around poetry, to find in this practice a way to talk about themselves and the world we share. As I travel around the country leading workshops and performing poetry, I hear from so many poets and organizers that they know workshops are important and would love to run them but don't know where to begin, or they begin and soon run out of material or time to commit to creating new workshops.

This model also seeks to refute the idea that poetry must be taught from a hierarchical perspective, that only an elitely educated few can access its secrets and unpack them for others.

No. Poems are made things, invented by regular people, and any one of us can pick them up, pull them apart, and have valid thoughts and opinions as to how and why they do the magic they do. In this way, poems are not puzzles to be solved, but a means of transmitting and sharing that can teach us how we can enable others to access and share their own experiences, imaginings, brutalities, ecstasies, and more.

This book contains all the information you need to run a community-based writing workshop. This includes 24 complete workshop plans, each of which includes an introductory question, a sample poem, discussion questions, and a writing exercise. It's my hope that this is enough to build a solid foundation for a workshop series that can flourish long after these plans are exhausted, and that you can adapt the practices included in this book to fit your unique facilitation style and the needs of the community that blossoms around it.

Muriel Rukeyser wrote, "The universe is made of stories, not of atoms." When we share stories, personal or personae, lived or dreamed, we build a universe together. When we do so through poetry, we are given a fleet of artistic permissions as well as feeling-containers, forms and structures through which we can introduce ourselves to the world and each other.

It's my highest hope that this book will enable more and more people in more and more places to build a better universe for us all. Thank you for being here, for making space for this magic to ignite, for all of our voices to gather.

CHAPTER TWO

# *Against Dismissiveness, Toward Curiosity*

I entered grad school knowing two things for certain: I loved poetry, and I couldn't stand Emily Dickinson.

Admittedly, my exposure to Emily Dickinson's work was limited to say the least, consisting entirely of anthologized poems and the weekly ritual of singing "Because I could not stop for death" to the tune of "The Yellow Rose of Texas" at the end of a local open mic.

In my first year of the MFA program, I expressed my distaste for Dickinson to a professor who, after dropping her shoulders and narrowing her eyes in either despair or distaste, pushed the left side of her signature mane back with a deliberate hand, leaned to me and said, "You are allowed to *dislike* Emily Dickinson, but you are not allowed not to *understand* Emily Dickinson."

———

When I was a sophomore in high school, a new girl moved into the neighborhood. She had a nose ring, blue hair, and a palpable disdain for everything. My mother, quite uncharacteristically, tried to insist that we become friends. I didn't like her. I explained this to my mother who said something about judging books by covers and guilted me into at least riding the bus with her a few times.

New Girl's dislike of everything included me, so we managed to avoid each other for the most part, despite our mothers' efforts. About six months later, I was sitting in the school pick-up/drop-off area waiting for my ride to the orthodontist when an ambulance blew in and New Girl was carried out on a stretcher: bad acid trip during lunch period, possible overdose, reliable student sources reported.

⁓

When we meet a poem that doesn't fit our aesthetic—that is too abstract or too narrative or too political or too minutely descriptive of the bark of an old oak tree—we often say "this is not a good poem" or "I don't like this poem" or "this poem has little or nothing to teach me."

But what if we approach the poem on its own terms? What if we assume that the poet who formed it and put it out in the world did so with great purpose and focused effort? What if we begin with *curiosity* instead of criticism?

If we do this, we can discover things outside our original expectations. Beginning from curiosity is relatively common practice in academic settings and others where groups of people gather to analyze published work and learn from it, but it's equally applicable when we approach poems in workshop settings, open mics, in slams, and so forth.

There's a parallel to this in human interaction. Ideally, we do not meet someone and immediately consider what we would change about them. Ideally, we assume positive intent on their part, that they are who they are intentionally and have shaped their lives and the way they move through the world not to injure or offend us but because it is an authentic (at least to them) representation of who they are.

If we encounter a person who is brash and seemingly sure of everything, robust in their opinions, and our aesthetic is for a softer, more inquisitive, gentler person, we may immediately think "I don't like this person" or "this is not a good person" or "this person has nothing to teach me."

But if we go forth in relationship with curiosity—if we ask why this person sets off in us these feelings, how they connect with parts of ourselves in shadow or light, disgust or desire, we can see them as a teacher and potentially make different choices.

~~~

Certainly, not every person needs to become our intimate companion, nor every poem have a place in our beloved library. Not every person or every poem is even "good," though "good" is less important in this framework than "transformative" or "teaching."

Emily Dickinson taught me to dig into abstraction and to trust even what I couldn't fully intellectually comprehend but could feel. And while I still don't belong to the Emily Dickinson fan club, understanding her work opened the door to my reading and loving Li-Young Lee's work, Anne Carson's work, Jorie Graham's work—the work of poets whose work treads a more fantastic terrain than I was previously open to encountering.

New Girl down the block didn't get to teach me anything because I decided there was nothing to learn. But 10 years later I was the one with blue hair and piercings, and I wonder what became of her.

What makes some poems worthy of our assuming they were created with intent? What makes some people worthy of our pushing past our prejudices? These are questions that go beyond aesthetics and move into the arena of why we assign value to what and to whom.

It's only when we are able to meet people and poems on their terms, rather than ours, that we are able to apprehend their magic. This is what we strive to do in all Gathering Voices workshops. *We start with curiosity.*

We begin with the assumption that every person and every poem we encounter has something to teach us. What a heavenly laboratory that makes this planet. What a gift.

# CHAPTER THREE

# The Gathering Voices Approach

I n the last chapter, I talked about curiosity as the foundational approach to the work that takes place within a Gathering Voices workshop. This chapter goes into greater detail around how that plays out in the workshop setting and lays out the other three fundamental practices: receptivity, joy, and rigor. I'll also talk about the three central Gathering Voices Commitments, in which these practices are summarized and translated into action.

## THE FUNDAMENTAL PRACTICES

### Curiosity

Many writing workshops are based on the explicit or implicit belief that poems brought to the group by participants are broken things in need of fixing or incomplete things in need of completion. The Gathering Voices approach asserts that as much, if not more, can be learned by discussing poems—ALL poems, at any stage of development—as works to be unpacked, examined, even debated. We begin by assuming that all the choices in a poem have been made purposefully, and we discuss how they affect us as readers.

We also strive toward curiosity and inquiry rather than declarations of personal taste or preference. Questions and inquiry open the discussion, where declarations tend to close down the room. Remember that we are here not just to improve these particular poems, but to build community and to strengthen the intellectual and artistic muscles that allow us to query the world around us and from that make personally and societally significant art.

For example, when someone states "I despise poems written in the second person" or makes a broad declaration such as "anytime there is a question in a poem, the poet is avoiding something and should just answer the question instead," the conversation often stalls. Other participants are presented with the options of disagreeing with the declaration or simply letting it stand—either way, the flow of discussion is disrupted and must be re-established.

Instead, consider an inquiry-based approach, focused on what is happening in the poem being discussed. The participant might say, "I wonder what would happen if this poem were written in first person—it seems to me that it would make it more immediate and personal" or "I feel like this being in second person puts a distance between the speaker and the content that isn't well-defined—if it were in third person, I think I'd understand that distance more."

This approach is modeled by the workshop facilitator (and, ideally, regular workshop participants) throughout the workshop, in discussing both the published poems and those brought to workshop by participants.

This inquiry-based approach helps to combat the risk of all poems coming out of a group sounding alike; as groupthink emerges, certain aesthetics get petrified into place, and discussion veers into "good poem" vs. "bad poem" territory.

Curiosity is also a way to combat cultural and personal bias—each of us comes to poetry with a set of understandings, expectations, ideas about what it means for a poem to be "good" based on what we've read, heard, been taught, or imagined. Rather than use these measurements, which may or may not apply to other people's poems, we inquire. We share how the writer's choices impact us as readers, and we listen to how those choices affected other people in the room. In this way, we learn instead of striving to prove ourselves learned or insightful or smart. We grow, together.

## Receptivity

This brings us to the second practice: *receptivity*. The flipside of all the effort we put into approaching poems from a curiosity standpoint, using inquiry instead of critique, is the willingness of the poet to receive that input.

Feedback provided in this way is a gift, and participants who choose to bring their work to the group for discussion should be prepared to receive it.

This is not to say that the writer should be expected to implement every piece of input they receive—indeed, the Gathering Voices style of discussion will often produce contradictory suggestions—but a willingness to hear and consider is crucial.

Part of your job as the facilitator is to listen closely to the feedback being provided and help to synthesize what's being offered to the writer. For example, one participant may suggest cutting the poem to just the third stanza and another may recommend keeping all parts of the poem but rearranging the order of the stanzas. As the facilitator, you can draw these threads together and remind the poet and the group that such input is helpful in allowing the poet to see the multiple paths they could take in moving the poem forward, providing the writer an opportunity to experiment and play. You might even have a third option to offer.

One note here about the facilitator's role: it's easy to become excited and want to offer all kinds of insight and input into the poem, but your primary role is to ensure that within the limited time the group is together, people have the opportunity to speak and be heard, to connect. This community-building is more important than any suggestion you have for a poem, no matter how brilliant. The less hierarchical a space you can build and maintain, the more powerful your Gathering Voices community will be.

It's also helpful to remind the poets who've brought their work to the group that sometimes a suggestion for changing something in a poem may not be precisely right but point to an area of their work that could use attention. I often share the fact that one of my poet friends who reads much of my work is almost always wrong about exactly what I should do with a poem but always right when he says something needs to be done about a particular aspect.

Here are two stories that help to illuminate the necessity and challenges of receptivity:

One poet had been coming to workshop for several months before she brought a poem of her own to be discussed by the group. After a lively conversation among the rest of the participants, when she was asked whether she had any final questions for the group, she declared that the poem had already been published, she thought it was perfect, and she had no intention of making any changes to it.

As the facilitator, I had to express dismay to the group that I hadn't been clear enough about only bringing poems for which we were seeking feedback, and apologize for that. Privately, I had to explain to the poet how hurtful it was to members of the group to have shared their ideas and suggestions only to be told that she wasn't interested in any of it and had wasted their time and energy.

By contrast, another poet came to workshop at a friend's recommendation, insisting that he wasn't really a poet, just had these small writings he did once in a while. He regularly volunteered poems for discussion, always listened closely to people's feedback, and offered insightful input on theirs. Within a year, he'd been accepted to an MFA in poetry program, now has two published full-length collections, and remains an active participant in workshops.

**Joy**

And this brings us to the third practice: JOY, which deserves all-caps treatment.

Joy in the work, joy in the community. Rare is the person who gets rich off of poetry, and almost as rare is the person who makes a living from writing it. We come to poetry for many things, and I would argue that important among them is joy. The same is true for community. We come together to make change, to lift each other up, to find commonality, to be challenged—and to remember and reinvent joy.

The world is a difficult place for anyone with sense and sensitivity enough to write poems. We've got to celebrate to survive and, in my opinion, the best way to do that is together.

**Rigor**

Finally, rigor.

At first blush, this practice might seem out of place in a workshop focused on building community as much as on building poems. But in rigor, in dedicated and sustained effort, we can find joy, as anyone who has mastered a new language, run a marathon, written a book, or otherwise surmounted major internal and external barriers will attest. The practices of curiosity and receptivity require the balance of rigor. In order for workshops to be more than poetry parties, we need to be committed to our own growth and that of other people.

Of course, rigor looks different for everyone. Some people will attend every minute of every workshop, put their name in the bowl every time in hope of having their poem examined, and come every time with a marked-up copy of the discussion poem. For some people, rigor looks like managing their social anxiety enough to leave their home and come to a room full of relative strangers.

What's important is not the form that rigor takes, but that there's a basic understanding that the workshop space is a workspace—full of joy and curiosity and receptivity, which makes it sacred work. Work to be honored and respected, where we honor and respect each other, the vulnerability it takes to engage meaningfully with art, and the time we've chosen to dedicate to poetry together.

## THE COMMITMENTS

Three essential commitments provide a guide for participant engagement, a way to check in when things seem like they may be going wrong, and help to ensure a space that is both challenging and safe for all involved.

Because these commitments are intended to guide the way participants interact as well as the way you facilitate the group, it's crucial that people receive this information before they arrive. Send them out via email when someone signs up for your mailing list, again with the workshop confirmation, and make sure to cover them in the workshop itself.

Whether you post them on the wall, read them aloud to the group, have a volunteer read them aloud, or some combination of these practices, the key is to create an environment of shared understanding. That way, if and when conflicts or concerns arise, you can refer to the commitments as an agreed-upon guide to appropriate participant behavior.

## Gathering Voices Commitments

(1) We value the potential, the experience, and the perspective each person brings. This is reflected in our words, actions, and attitudes.

(2) We approach poems not as broken things in need of fixing, nor as objects of like or dislike, but as subjects of study and analysis, artworks whose possibilities we get to unpack.

(3) We come ready to work, eager to engage, and committed to creating a positive, challenging environment for everyone.

# CHAPTER FOUR

# *Notes on Poetic Jargon*

S o much of our education and socialization around poetry is designed to, or at least has the effect of, distancing us from it and convincing us that we need advanced degrees and extensive memorized lists of terminology to have a chance of understanding it.

Here's what I believe and what I say in workshops: *if you can read, you can read poetry.*

The force behind a poem, what drives its creation, is indeed mysterious. But its construction, its structure, its components, and how those interact to make a whole poem—that can all be analyzed, pulled apart, and discussed. And to do that work, it is helpful to have some shared language.

I often describe poetic terms as *shortcuts.* It's definitely faster to say "I'm interested in how the enjambment across line breaks in the second stanza contributes to the pace of the poem" than "I'm interested in how the fact that sentences continue over the ends of lines in the part of the poem after the first big white space makes me move quickly through it." But both get the job done. Both communicate the impact of the poet's structural choices on this particular reader.

As the facilitator, you get to make choices about how and when you interject poetic terminology into the workshop discussion, and how and when you use it yourself. This becomes less important when you've established that at any point, anyone in the group should feel free to throw a hand up and ask for clarification or definition.

A particularly effective way of establishing this comfort level is to ask questions yourself—you don't have to prove yourself an expert in order to be a great facilitator. If you don't know a term that someone uses, ask! And if you sense that someone in the group doesn't know what a term means, you can ask on behalf of the group.

This itself can lead to more interesting, in-depth discussions of poems. While poetic terminology can be useful, it can also lead to commentary that lacks actual substance and instead simply strings together terminology that sounds impressive but doesn't advance the conversation.

For example, if someone in my workshop were to say, "I note that there's a caesura just before the volta in the penultimate line of the poem." I would say something like, "Oh cool—so we're looking at the second to last line of the poem. Can you talk to us about what *caesura* and *volta* mean? And, how does the poet's use of those affect your reading of the poem?"

In this way, we're all learning together, and the person offering this thought has the opportunity to go further with that thought, moving the discussion along without alienating the person with the extensive poetic vocabulary or anyone in the group who doesn't know or remember what those terms mean.

Remember that even though you are the facilitator, *you don't need to know everything*. Not knowing allows you to model unabashed asking, based in curiosity about the language being used to describe the poem as well as the poem itself.

This applies equally to words used within a poem, as well as any historical, literary, mythological or other kind of context. Let's not assume that everyone is familiar with Greek mythology or the Bible or the imagists or the Black Arts Movement—again, coming from a place of curiosity lets you, the facilitator, ask questions and model this inquiry-based approach.

For example, if someone brought a poem entitled "Samson," a question you might ask is, "Does anyone know the Biblical story of Samson and Delilah?" followed by a question about what significance, if any, the group feels it has for the poem.

There are many excellent books on craft, techniques, revision practices, and poetic forms in the world. This book does not seek to be one of them. However, a brief glossary of the aspects of poetic technique, form, and craft that most often arise in workshops may be helpful, and is included below.

We'll use this poem fragment as an example in many of these definitions.

> Remember, love, fire needs air, but air
> does not need fire. History can find you
> anywhere. In traffic, at dinner, and absolutely
>
> at the bottom of the bottle, though likely
> you won't remember. You're lucky
> to be here. Say *Thank you.*

*Line break*: the place where one line ends and another begins. In the example poem above, the lines break on the words "air," "you," "absolutely," "likely," "lucky," and "you."

*White space*: the space on the printed page that does not include words. Sometimes referred to as "empty space" or "blank space."

*Stanza*: a stanza in poetry is similar to a paragraph in prose; it is the block of lines before a break. Some poems have stanza breaks, and some poems are only one stanza. In the example poem, the stanzas break at the words "absolutely" and "you."

*Couplet*: a two-line stanza.

*Tercet*: a three-line stanza. As shown in example on previous page.

*Quatrain*: a four-line stanza.

*Quintet*: a five-line stanza.

*Sestet*: a six-line stanza.

*Septet*: a seven-line stanza.

*Octave*: an eight-line stanza.

*Enjambment*: the continuation of a sentence or clause over a line break or stanza break. The sentences in the example poem are enjambed across the line breaks and the first stanza break.

*Direct address*: the technique of speaking directly to someone in a poem. The example poem uses direct address by speaking to a "you."

*Speaker*: we can't assume that the speaker in the poem is the same person as the poet. One way to make this clear is to refer to the speaker in the poem rather than the writer when discussing the content of the poem. For example, in discussing the example poem, one might say, "The speaker in this poem seems to know a lot about the person being addressed, and feels free to say things that might offend that person."

*Point of view*: generally speaking, there are three options with regard to the perspective from which the poem is written: first person, second person, and third person. *First person* normally uses the words "I" or "we," and indicates that the speaker in the poem is speaking from their own perspective. *Second person* involves the use of the word "you," which may mean the speaker or may mean a generalized other—in the example poem, if the word "love" were excluded from the first line, we might interpret the poem as being written in the second person, and in that case the pronoun "you" could be interpreted as referring directly to the speaker. In *third person*, we find pronouns such as "he," "she," "it," or "they"—the speaker is observing and reporting back.

*Epistle* or *epistolary poems*: a kind of poem that reads as a letter. Some actually begin with "Dear _____" but many do not.

*Persona poem*: a poem in which the speaker is explicitly indicated as not being the person who wrote the poem.

*Prose poem*: a poem without line breaks.

*Tense*: while English is full of complicated variations on tenses, generally within the workshop those discussed are the past (what has happened), present (what is happening now), and future (what will happen.)

*Diction*: the kind of language—including vocabulary, phrasing, grammatical structures, and linguistic style—used in a poem. In the example poem, the diction is similar to that of everyday speech—the vocabulary is fairly standard, as is the grammatical construction of the sentences. However, let's say the poem continued with lines such as, "In the tumult of your specious post-adolescenting, every bottle becomes spyglass. Every shot glass hypodermic." In that case, we might talk about the diction becoming *elevated*—raised to a different level from ordinary speech.

*Tone*: the speaker's attitude toward the subject or audience.

*Consonance*: the repetition of consonant sounds. This repetition can occur within words, across words, within phrases, sentences, stanzas, or whole poems. The words "can," "traffic," "Christmas," "likely," "lucky," and "thank" exhibit consonance in the example poem.

*Assonance*: the repetition of vowel sounds. This repetition can occur within words, across words, within phrases, sentences, stanzas, or whole poems. The words "remember," "needs," "need," "history," "anywhere," "absolutely," "likely," "lucky," "be," and "here" exhibit assonance in the example poem.

*Alliteration*: A special kind of consonance or assonance where repeated sounds occur at the beginning of the words. In the fourth line of the example poem, "bottom" and "bottle" alliterate.

*Imagery*: parts of a poem that invoke sight.

*Metaphor*: a comparison that is made between two essentially unlike things without using words such as "like," "as," or "than." For example, "all the world's a stage."

*Simile*: a comparison between two essentially unlike things using words such as "like," "as," or "than." For example, "my love is like the sun."

*Connotation*: the non-literal meaning of a word—its suggested or implied meaning. Often this involves its emotional associations, cultural context, or other sub-surface meanings.

*Denotation*: the literal, dictionary definition of a word.

*Personification*: attributing human characteristics or qualities to a thing, an idea or an animal.

*Epigraph*: a brief piece of text, generally borrowed from another writer. This is usually placed after the title but before the body of the poem. Some books also have epigraphs at the beginning of the book and/or the beginning of each section.

For those seeking a solid initial grounding in poetic terminology and practice, I highly recommend Mary Oliver's *A Poetry Handbook* (Houghton Mifflin Harcourt, 1994).

# CHAPTER FIVE

# *Nuts and Bolts: How to Run a Gathering Voices Workshop, Start to Finish*

Gathering Voices workshops are run by facilitators, not teachers. What this means is that your role as the leader of this group is to provide the space, structure, materials, and support for its members to explore, discover, create, and connect.

You are not here to impart lessons or teach skills, though lessons may be learned and skills developed. What you offer Gathering Voices workshop participants is a clear set of expectations, an open and inquisitive approach, and a structure designed to honor and amplify the insights and intelligence of the individual participants and the group as a synergistic whole.

Common worries for the workshop leader include how they will manage participants who are overly talkative or deathly quiet, whether or not people will like the poem they've brought for discussion, and how to make sure the workshop runs and ends on time.

For the workshop participant, concerns often arise from not knowing what the norms for engagement are, not knowing what's going to happen next, and fear of saying something stupid.

The workshop plans in this book include discussion questions that can help address some of those concerns. Asking open-ended questions without academic jargon helps, as does the practice described below of always beginning with the very general question of, "What do you notice about the poem?" and inviting participants to start by stating the obvious:

the poem has four stanzas, the title is only one word, the poem is only one long sentence, and so on.

Approaching poems as *subjects of study and analysis*, rather than objects of like or dislike, helps to allay another fear. Maybe everyone in the workshop hates the published poem brought in for discussion—fine! We can learn as much, if not more, from art that disturbs us as from art that delights us.

A discussion based on what we like is a very limited discussion. A discussion focused on how a poem works, what choices the author made, how making other choices would affect the poem, and why the author might have made a particular choice, is a much richer, more productive one.

Set structure and clear expectations create space for participants—and workshop leaders—to take positive risks and engage at their own pace and comfort level. Knowing that, let's get started!

**Before the Workshop**

The tone and expectation-setting for the workshop begins before anyone sets foot in the gathering place. Requesting RSVPs not only allows you, the workshop leader, to estimate how many individuals will attend and plan accordingly, but also allows you to connect with each participant at least once before the workshop date.

At least one day in advance of the workshop, send out a confirmation email that includes:

- the published poem to be discussed
- the practices and commitments summary (included as Appendix C)
- a summary of the workshop plan (group discussion of a published poem, writing time using an exercise drawing on the discussed

poem, and group critique of three poems volunteered by workshop participants)

- a reminder to bring something to write on or with (computer, paper/pen, etc.)
- a reminder to bring an appropriate number of copies of their poem if they would like to have it discussed by the group
- an invitation to bring snacks and drinks to share with the group
- a reminder of the workshop arrival, start, and end times

A sample confirmation email is included in the appendix of this book.

There is also the question of your preparation to lead the workshop. In addition to selecting the workshop plan you intend to use, you'll want to spend some time with the poem and the discussion questions. Note what questions come up for you as you read the poem, and thoughts on how you might answer the discussion questions. Remember that your job is not to become an expert on the poem, but to be comfortable enough with it to move the conversation along and guide the group in unpacking the poem at hand.

## THE WORKSHOP ITSELF

**3-hour workshop structure:**

- Arrival and socializing: 30-minute window
- Introductions: 15 to 30 minutes
- Published poem discussion: 45 minutes
- Writing exercise: 15 minutes
- Break: 15 minutes
- Discussion of three poems from the group: 45 minutes
  (or 60 minutes if introductions only ran 15 minutes)

If possible, provide a half-hour arrival window before the workshop begins. This serves two purposes: one, it offers participants an opportunity to connect with each other outside of the workshop structure itself, and two, it facilitates your ability to begin at the clearly stated start time.

A note on timeliness: I had a workshop professor in grad school who would stop mid-sentence and silently watch as anyone arriving late made the long trip around the enormous round table to the only empty seat. As torturous as it seemed at the time, her critical question—*What is it that was more important than the time of your fellow students?*—makes a great deal of sense. As soon as the workshop begins, a world is created. Of course things happen and people are occasionally unavoidably late, but establishing a practice of starting on time and addressing it privately but promptly if a pattern of late arrival emerges is crucial to maintaining the integrity of the workshop.

Put out two bowls or jars: one with slips of paper on which people can write their names if they'd like to have a poem discussed by the group, and one for donations.

A note on donations: this is, of course, an individual choice. The language I use is that there is a suggested donation of X amount, with no one turned away for lack of funds. While money shouldn't be a barrier to participation, it's my opinion that artists of all kinds should be paid for their work, and facilitating workshops is, indeed, work. You've purchased this book, made your space available or arranged for another space, prepared and promoted and organized, and that's work.

One more thing before we get to the workshop itself: *food!* As the workshop leader, you can set any parameters you like (i.e., no alcohol, only vegetarian dishes, nothing with peanuts, no purple food, etc.), but encouraging people to bring snacks and drinks to share contributes importantly to the sense of community and connectedness we are aiming for in this process.

## Workshop Part 1: Welcome and Introductory Question

Each workshop plan in this book includes an introductory question. These generally relate to the content of the published poem to be discussed, but their primary purpose is to help build community through familiarity. The questions also provide an early opportunity for participants to practice vulnerability and boundary setting, as they decide how personal an answer to offer the group. In addition, the introductory question gently sets the precedent for everyone speaking in turn during the workshop.

To start the workshop, I will generally go first—reminding people of my name, giving my gender pronouns, and answering the introductory question. I'll then ask for a volunteer to share their name, an answer to the introductory question, and *if they like*, what their pronouns are (she, he, they, or something else.) They can then pass to their left or their right, and each participant around the room will do the same.

A note on pronouns: no one should be required to share their pronouns, but it is important to provide the space in which this information can be offered. You can model this as the facilitator by sharing yours, if you are comfortable doing so.

Depending on the size of the group, the introduction activity will likely run 15 to 30 minutes. If you have a large and/or talkative group, you may need to ask them to limit their responses to just a sentence or two.

## Workshop Part 2: Discussion of the Published Poem

On to the poetry! You've sent the poem out at least a day in advance, but it's rarely safe to assume that people will have printed the poem out, let alone reviewed it before the workshop. If possible, have printed copies available. And pens—there's always someone without a pen.

Ask for two volunteers to read the poem aloud to the group. Many of the poems included in this book are quite dense and lend themselves to multiple interpretations—and therefore lively discussions—so hearing them more than once, and in more than one voice, is useful in starting the conversation.

Remind the group of two primary guidelines for the discussion:

1. Focus as much as possible on what *choices* were made in the making of the poem—assuming the poet did everything on purpose, what is the impact of those choices on you, the reader? Let's talk about this instead of what we like or dislike.
2. Stay within the boundaries of the poem—focus on unpacking the poem instead of talking about how the inclusion of an elephant reminds you of this one time when you went to the circus as a child, and got sick off cotton candy. Unless that illuminates something about the poem! Then by all means talk about the elephant.

Launch the discussion with the question, "What do you notice about the poem?" and invite participants to start by stating the obvious: the poem has four stanzas, the title is only one word, the poem is only one long sentence, and so on.

One thing to note is that while we often assume poetry to be autobiographical, this is not necessarily the case. So while discussing this published poem and in the later portion where the group is discussing poems by people in the room, you may need to remind participants to talk about *the speaker* in the poem, not assuming this is the same person as the writer of the poem. For example, even if I know that the writer of a poem identifies as female, I cannot assume that the speaker in a poem she has written is female. I have to look to the poem itself for indications that this is the case, if it is significant.

The discussion questions that are included in each workshop plan are not intended to be a comprehensive list, but instead a series of jumping-off points, ways to initiate conversation and move the group into exploration of the poem. Read through the questions before the workshop and think about what other questions you're interested in investigating with the group.

Poetry-specific vocabulary and vernacular is often a primary barrier to people reading, loving, and apprehending poetry. To avoid or manage this, as the facilitator you can gently ask for explanations of any "ten-dollar words" that get tossed around (caesura, consonance, cinquain, etc.)—whether you know them or not, it's useful to unpack this language and get at its relevance to the poem at hand. (See Chapter 4 for some of this terminology.)

To close, ask if there are any final thoughts or comments people would like to make, particularly those who haven't yet shared. If you are using the three-hour workshop model, this portion of the workshop should run about 45 minutes.

**Workshop Part 3: Writing Exercise**

Once you've closed discussion of the published poem, it's time for some writing.

The exercises included in each workshop plan draw on some aspect or aspects of the poem the group has just spent time discussing. Many of the exercises are very structured and involve interaction among participants. This is designed to get people out of their usual writing patterns, introduce a sense of play and positive risk, and give participants a solid launching point for their writing.

In introducing the writing exercise, it's helpful to remind participants that the goal is not to come up with a fully realized poem in the next 10 to 15 minutes, but to use this time to get started, to take chances, to have fun with the writing and see what happens.

Writing during this time is certainly not required, but participants shouldn't start side conversations or do anything that would distract those who are using the time to write. Introduction of the exercise and any group components generally runs three to five minutes, and participants take about 10 minutes to write.

**Workshop Part 4: The Break**

After the writing time, participants are free to spend about 10 minutes mingling, sharing their writing with each other if they like, partaking of some of the food and drink they've brought to share, and so on. Participants are welcome to continue writing during this time if they like, but the injunction against distraction is lifted.

During this break, pull three names from the hat—these are the writers whose poems will be discussed in the final portion of workshop.

**Workshop Part 5: Group Discussion of Participant Poems**

The order for the poems to be discussed can be the order in which they were pulled from the bowl, alphabetical by poet, or by poets volunteering. If one of the poems is particularly long, I find that it's best to look at that poem first or second, rather than saving it for last.

As copies of the poem are being passed around, ask the poet if there is any kind of input in particular they would like from the group. Have someone who is not the author read the poem to the group, then offer the poet the opportunity to read it aloud.

As with the published poems, it's often useful to hear the poem more than once, and in more than one voice. Hearing the poem read by someone who did not write it frequently provides illumination around possible interpretations, and prevents the author's performance from coloring the initial impression of the poem. Hearing the poem subsequently read by its author can offer insights into different interpretations and levels of meaning that may or may not be accessible in the written text.

The poem's author becomes a "fly on the wall" during the discussion—they cannot offer additional information, details, background, etc. once they have read the poem aloud. This supports the participants in focusing on and querying the poem as it is printed on the page, rather than seeking answers from the poet.

Remind the participants that we use essentially the same approach in this discussion as we did with the published poem in the first part of the workshop. We focus on the impact of the poet's choices, places where different choices could be made and how that would affect the poem, and things we notice about the poem's content, structure, and presentation on the page.

As with the published poems, we do not assume that the author of the poem is also the speaker in the poem. Not every poem is autobiographical. So in discussing the poem, it's important to focus on what we learn or know *based on the poem itself*, striving to avoid conjecture or layering meaning onto the poem based on what we know or believe about the writer.

Before the poem is read aloud, ask the writer if they want any particular kind of feedback on the poem (focusing particularly on the physical layout, or thoughts on the ending specifically, for example), or want to provide information about it that is not present in the poem (such as it being part of a series).

Recognizing that the poet is in the room and that the act of bringing one's work to the group is a vulnerable one, ask the group to begin affirmatively. Start by asking about what stands out to participants in a positive way about the poem, and request that they save questions, critiques, or points of confusion until one or two affirming comments have been made.

Here are some sample questions it can be helpful to ask about poems brought by workshop participants:

- What do you notice about the rhythm of the poem?
- Is anything in the poem repeated—either full words or sounds? How does that affect you as a reader/listener?
- How does this poem engage the five senses—smell, touch, taste, sight, hearing?
- Does the tone or feeling of the poem change or remain the same throughout?
- To whom is the speaker in this poem speaking? Why?
- What line would you say is the "heart" of this poem?
- How does the point of view (first person, second person, third person) in the poem affect you as the reader?
- What kind of language is used in this poem—is it written in the way you would expect to hear someone speak, or is the language heightened or elevated? How does that interact with the content of the poem?
- What do you notice about the physical structure of the poem—how it looks on the page? How does that match or create tension with the content of the poem?
- In what order is information offered up in this poem? What do we learn in each line, each stanza?
- How would this poem be different if it were read backward, last line up to the first?

- How would this poem be different if it were written in a different tense (past instead of present, present instead of future, etc.)?
- What would you say is the central feeling of this poem?
- Are there any places where you get stuck or lost in the poem? Can anyone in the group unpack/illuminate those places?
- What kind of work are the verbs doing in this poem?
- What role do objects play in this poem, if any?
- What question can you imagine this poem answering?

It can be useful to point out that the group having many questions about a poem is not necessarily a bad thing, and certainly not to be taken personally. Many of the world's greatest poems are discussed, analyzed, pulled apart, and critiqued endlessly.

Encourage participants to make notes on the printed poem if they like. It's likely that not everyone will have time to share all of their thoughts on each poem. Notes on the poem can be a great way to indicate small edits, such as changes in punctuation, lines or phrases that particularly stand out, or to thoughts on other poems or poets that come to mind when reading the poem at hand.

The discussion of each poem should run about 12 to 15 minutes. Part of your role as workshop leader is to make sure that each poem gets about the same amount of time and attention. You may want to ask for a volunteer to serve as the timekeeper for these discussion, so that no one gets shortchanged and the workshop can end on time.

To close the discussion of each poem, ask the group if there are any final comments, particularly from those who haven't shared their thoughts yet.

You may want to summarize some of what you've heard from the group in terms of suggestions, particularly if you see common threads or interesting divergences in opinion that could could send the poem in interesting or unexpected new directions.

Ask the poet if there's anything they want to ask or tell the group briefly before the group moves on to the next poem.

As described earlier in this book, a Gathering Voices discussion begins with a consideration of what the poem wants, and what we understand the poet's intent might be, rather than what we, the reader, want it to be. We approach with curiosity rather than criticism.

Our goal in these discussions is not to take other people's poems and make them into the poems we would write, but to analyze them with the same respect we give published, ostensibly "finished" poems and provide the poet with an opportunity to see engaged readers in action, analyzing, honoring, and seeking to understand the work that poet is putting out into the world. It is then up to the poet to take that information and consider what changes, if any, they want to make to the poem as a result.

It is also not our goal in these discussions to come to consensus or agreement on what a poem "means" or what the correct course of action is with regard to possible changes to the poem. A poem can contain multiple meanings, and sometimes the discussion comes down to whether it effectively bears the weight of its ambiguity. A poet may consider multiple right courses of action with a poem before settling on one that they feel best serves the poem—a beauty of the workshop setting is its ability to present multiple perspectives and possibilities for a poem.

These workshops are designed to be a place to experiment and discover options, which frees us from the need to find a "right answer" or agree on what should happen with a poem.

Essentially, the Gathering Voices workshop aims to create connections between individuals, broaden and deepen critical thought, facilitate positive risk-taking and artistic play, and open new worlds of possibility for poems and the people who write them.

CHAPTER SIX

# *Beyond the Basics*

This chapter provides insight and guidance related to the wraparound activities involved with starting and running an effective Gathering Voices workshop series.

**Outreach and Marketing**

The first thing a workshop needs is people! Great places to promote your workshop include local open mics and slams, book groups, bookstores, and coffee shops.

One thing people often assume about a writing workshop is that it will be three solid hours of discussing poems by people in the room. While there's nothing inherently wrong with this, it's different from a Gathering Voices workshop.

It can be helpful to emphasize to potential participants that because of the workshop structure, there is no pressure to bring your own work for discussion, immediately or ever. This provides space for even those who are interested in poetry but do not necessarily write it to join in the community and become active participants.

**Creating A Schedule**

Included in this book are 24 complete workshop plans. How you schedule these 24 workshops is of course entirely up to you and what works for your community. I have found that particularly when a workshop series is just beginning, it is helpful to establish some consistency so that people can plan their attendance.

## Building A Team

In the early years of offering Gathering Voices workshops, we would often have more than 30 people attend, which was too much for one facilitator. I was fortunate to have access to a space where we could split into two groups and to have community members able to take on facilitation for one of those groups.

This, too, is a matter of personal preference, but getting help promoting workshops, managing RSVPs, preparing and cleaning the space, and even facilitating workshops can help prevent burnout and keep your workshop going long beyond the span of the 24 sessions laid out in this book.

## Maintaining Boundaries

One thing I struggled with in my early years as a poetry organizer was the pressure to be friends with everyone who passed through the series I helped run. So I say to you as you embark on facilitating these workshops: you do not have to be everyone's friend. You can be kind and welcoming and supportive without also having to share all aspects of your life with everyone who comes to workshop. It does pay off to think about your boundaries before starting to run workshops; are you comfortable having people in your home? If so, in which parts? Are you good with people seeing the dirty dishes in your sink, or is the kitchen off-limits?

Timing may be an important boundary for you. I provide a half-hour window between earliest arrival and workshop start; up until that earliest arrival minute I may still be in my pajamas, or eating dinner, or just getting centered and ready for the presence of new energy in my space. In any case, that door doesn't open until the specified time.

You owe it to yourself and your participants to have and hold clear boundaries, and they owe it to you to respect those.

As the facilitator, you are taking on a leadership role. The people who come to your workshop are entrusting you with their art, their time, and their investment in community. Don't abuse it. Be deeply cautious about romantic involvement with people you meet through the workshops, and get very clear affirmative consent before engaging in romantic or sexual activities with the anyone you're leading.

For more information on affirmative consent, visit one of these resources:

http://www.loveisrespect.org/healthy-relationships/what-consent/
https://www.rainn.org/articles/what-is-consent

You may not feel that leading a free poetry workshop in the back room of the local coffee shop puts you in a position of power, but in certain ways, it does. As a facilitator, your role is to first ensure the emotional and physical safety of each individual in your sessions (including yourself), and then to ensure the safety of the community.

This applies as well to problematic or predatory behavior by individuals who come to your workshop. Hopefully you will never be confronted with a participant who is racist or sexist or commits micro aggressions or otherwise damages the space you have worked hard to create, but if you do, I hope that you will listen most closely to whoever has the least power in that situation, focusing first on hearing and protecting those who have been harmed, and seek support from others with experience and expertise in addressing such situations.

Whether it is through transformative justice approaches, mediation, and/or explicitly ensuring that an individual knows they are no longer welcome in your space, remember that you don't have to go it alone. The broader poetry community and the internet are full of resources and individuals who have gone through situations of problematic power dynamics and damaging behavior and come out the other side wiser and with established practices that can support you in this. Don't be afraid to reach out and ask for help.

## Making It Your Own

After six chapters telling you what to do down to the minute, it may seem strange to end with this. But make the workshop your own! The information contained in this book is designed to provide a scaffold on which you will construct and nurture your own learning community, your own gathering of voices. Every facilitator is different, and every gathering is different. You've come this far. It's going to be great.

CHAPTER SEVEN

# *The Workshops*

## Introduction

*Why these poems?*

The poems used in the workshop plans that follow have been selected for a variety of reasons. While I believe strongly in the benefits of reading poems from all eras, in a wide range of styles, and understanding the historical roots of the work we are creating now, the Gathering Voices workshops seek in part to balance academia's strong emphasis on the long– and highly revered dead ("the canon") by studying the work of poets alive and writing today.

Some of these poets are internationally renowned; others have yet to publish a full-length book. They represent a broad range of genders, racial and ethnic backgrounds, and aspects of queerness. The poems themselves have been selected to offer a range of perspectives, content areas, stylistic approaches, and writing techniques.

Choosing poems to bring to workshop for discussion is very much a balancing act. Some basic criteria are:

- Is it long enough to permit extensive discussion, but can be read aloud within two to three minutes?
- Is it challenging enough to generate interesting conversation, but not so experimental or abstract as to bore or stymie participants who are new to poetry?
- Are there aspects of the poem that workshop regulars are

particularly interested in right now? (For example, great endings or the extended metaphor or tackling big political issues?)

- Does it offer some variety from the last poem we discussed, either in style, content, or writer's identity?

*Why are the writing exercises structured the way they are?*

The exercises included in this book are extensive, interactive, and often disruptive to people's ordinary ways of writing.

The extensiveness of the exercises is designed to help move us past brain freeze, beyond the terror of the blank page. Especially for new writers or seasoned poets battling writers' block, having a structure to write into, a word or phrase bank to draw from, and/or a concept to tackle can be incredibly helpful with just getting started.

And that's all we are trying to do in the brief freewrite period of the Gathering Voices workshop—get started. It's rare that anyone manages to crank out a complete draft, though it does happen. It can be helpful to be explicit about this and help set a tone of exploration and discovery.

So often we approach the page with a kind of dread or heaviness, weighted down by the idea that for our precious time to be well-spent, it must produce a great work of art. This is a terrible burden to place on a rough draft, so these exercises try to lift that by encouraging us to engage in writing as play, to send the inner critic out for snacks while the draft is written.

On a more subtle level, many of the prompt activities are designed to move our writing past the surface level, to go beyond the initial thought or feeling into the place where transformation and transcendence happen. Many also help us practice some of the techniques used so expertly in the discussion poems.

The interactivity of the exercises is related to the community-based nature of the workshops. Writing is for many of us primarily a solitary activity, and these exercises offer us an opportunity to engage with each other before we settle into our individual spaces to write.

Finally, the disruptive nature of many of these prompts is based on a bias toward the unexpected in poems. Poems, like life, are most transcendent when they offer surprises, when they go unexpected places, when we could not have known where we would end up when this experience began. Intentionally disrupting our practice lets us exercise neglected or untried writing muscles, taking the work to new and potentially transformative levels.

# BECAUSE IT'S SUMMER

## Ocean Vuong

you ride your bike to the park bruised
with 9pm the maples draped with plastic bags
shredded from days in the cornfield
freshly razed & you've lied
about where you're going you're supposed
to be out with a woman you can't find
a name for but he's waiting
in the baseball field behind the dugout
flecked with newports torn condoms
he's waiting with sticky palms & mint
on his breath a cheap haircut
& his sister's levis
stench of piss rising from wet grass
it's june after all & you're young
until september he looks different
from his picture but it doesn't matter
because you kissed your mother
on the cheek before coming
this far because the fly's dark slit is enough
to speak through the zipper a thin scream
where you plant your mouth
to hear the sound of birds
hitting water snap of elastic
waistbands four hands quickening
into dozens: a swarm of want you wear
like a bridal veil but don't
deserve it: the boy &
his loneliness the boy who finds you

beautiful only because you're not
a mirror because you don't have
enough faces to abandon you've come
this far to be no one & it's june
until morning you're young until a pop song
plays in a dead kid's room water spilling in
from every corner of summer & you want
to tell him *it's okay* that the night is also a grave
we climb out of but he's already fixing
his collar the cornfield a cruelty steaming
with manure you smear your neck with
lipstick you dress with shaky hands
you say *thank you thank you thank you*
because you haven't learned the purpose
of *forgive me* because that's what you say
when a stranger steps out of summer
& offers you another hour to live

# INTRODUCTORY QUESTION

What is one lie you have told someone who raised you?

(This can be on any scale—a white lie like "yes I ate my vegetables" or something larger.)

# SAMPLE DISCUSSION QUESTIONS

What stands out to you about the poem? What do you notice?

How does the title also being the first line of the poem affect your entrance into the poem?

What line would you say is the heart of the poem?

How do you see the five senses being used in this poem—smell, touch, taste, hearing, sight?

Who are the characters in this poem? What do we learn about each of them?

Each workshop plan in this book begins with an introductory question to be presented to the group and answered aloud by each participant. These generally relate to the content of the published poem to be discussed, but their primary purpose is to help build community through familiarity. The questions also provide an early opportunity for participants to practice vulnerability and boundary setting, as they decide how personal an answer to offer the group. In addition, the introductory question gently sets the precedent for everyone speaking in turn during the workshop.

These discussion questions
are not intended to be a
comprehensive list, but
instead a series of jumping-
off points, ways to initiate
conversation and move
the group into exploration
of the poem. Read through
the questions before the
workshop and think about
what other questions you're
interested in investigating
with the group.

How does the poet distinguish between
what seems to be and what is in
this poem?

How does the poet's use of the second
person ("you" meaning "I") affect your
experience of the poem?

How does use of punctuation and
capitalization in the poem affect you as
a reader?

What is the role of time in the poem—
months that are named, the idea of being
young, movement between past, present,
and future tenses?

How would this poem feel different
to read if it were arranged with
stanza breaks?

What is the role of wanting or desire in
the poem? What desires are overt, and
which hidden?

*Before the workshop, print out copies of the worksheet and cut enough slips of paper for each participant to receive three, each one large enough for a sentence. Put out three bowls.*

*Read these instructions aloud to the workshop participants, giving them time to carry out each instruction before moving on to the next one. Distribute the slips of paper, three per participant.*

Today's exercise works best when you don't think too much! Don't worry about being right or smart or poetic. Just go with whatever comes to mind as you carry out the following steps.

(1) Write a full sentence that is an obvious lie (for example, the sky is green, a penguin is an octopus, etc.) on one slip of paper. Put that in the first bowl.

(2) Write down a question, any question, on the second slip of paper. Put that in the second bowl.

(3) This step is in two parts. Part one: write down a physical location. Part two: list three characteristics of that location. Now, put that paper in the third bowl.

*Once everyone has put their pieces of paper in the bowls:*

(4) Pull a location slip from the third bowl. This is where your poem (or some part of your poem) will take place. Now pull a piece of paper from each of the other bowls.

(5) Time to freewrite! You have a worksheet with a series of instructions.

On the paper provided, freewrite using the instructions on the worksheet as you wish—going in order is encouraged, but it's your poem!"

Also, try not to worry too much about making sense or writing a great poem—the idea here is to let the automatic parts of your brain take over and have some fun. You may end up with a poem draft, or a series of lines, sentences, phrases, and concepts to play with the next time you sit down to write. Either is great!

*Following are a series of instructions for your freewrite. Let these be jumping-off points for your writing, mini-prompts to keep you going as the poem develops!*

Write a sentence about the location you pulled from the bowl, including one of the characteristics listed.

Write a sentence about a scent you've nearly forgotten starting with the phrase, "I almost forgot."

Within your freewrite, ask someone a question.

Write down the lie you pulled from the bowl.

Write a sentence that begins with, "When you lied about..."

Write a sentence about the location you pulled from the bowl, including another one of the characteristics listed on the paper.

Write a sentence that confesses that the something you've written was a lie, starting with, "I lied when I said..."

Write a sentence that explains why you lied.

Write down the question that you pulled from the bowl.

Write a sentence about the location you pulled from the bowl, including another one of the characteristics listed.

Write a sentence or two describing the shoes your conscience wears.

Within your freewrite, ask someone else a question.

Write a sentence that begins with "It is true that..."

Within your freewrite, thank someone for something.

# A COLORED GIRL WILL SLICE YOU IF YOU TALK WRONG ABOUT MOTOWN

## Patricia Smith

The men and women who coupled, causing us, first
arrived confounded. Surrounded by teetering towers
of *no, not now*, and *you shoulda known better*, they
cowered and built little boxes of Northern home,
crammed themselves inside, feasted on the familiar
of fat skin and the unskimmed, made gods of doors.
When we came—the same insistent bloody and question
we would have been down South—they clutched us,
plumped us on government cereal drenched in Carnation,
slathered our hair, faces, our fat wiggling arms and legs
with Vaseline. We shined like the new things we were.
The city squared its teeth, smiled oil, smelled the sour
each hour left at the corner of our mouths. Our parents
threw darts at the day. They romanced shut factories,
waged hot battle with skittering roaches and vermin,
lumbered after hunches. Their newborn children grew
like streetlights. We grew like insurance payments.
We grew like resentment. And since no tall sweet gum
thrived to offer its shouldered shade, no front porch
lesson spun wide to craft our wrong or righteous,

our parents loosed us into the crumble, into the glass,
into the hips of a new city. They trusted exploded
summer hydrants, scarlet licorice whips, and crumbling
rocks of government cheese to conjure a sort of joy,
trusted joy to school us in the woeful limits of jukeboxes
and moonwash. Freshly dunked in church water, slapped

away from double negatives and country ways, we were
orphans of the North Star, dutifully sacrificed, our young
bodies arranged on sharp slabs of boulevard. We learned
what we needed, not from our parents and their rumored
South, but from the gospel seeping through the sad gap
in Mary Wells's grin. Smokey slow-sketched pictures
of our husbands, their future skins flooded with white light,
their voices all remorse and atmospheric coo. Little Stevie
squeezed his eyes shut on the soul notes, replacing his
dark with ours. Diana was the bone our mamas coveted,
the flow of slip silver they knew was buried deep beneath
their rollicking heft. Every lyric, growled or sweet from
perfect brown throats, was instruction: *Sit pert, pout, and
seamed silk. Then watch him beg.* Every spun line was
consolation: *You're such a good girl. If he has not arrived,
he will.* Every wall of horn, every slick choreographed
swivel, threaded us with the rhythm of the mildly wild.
We slept with transistor radios, worked the two silver knobs,
one tiny earbud blocking out the roar of our parents' tardy
attempts to retrieve us. Instead, we snuggled with the Temps,
lined up five pretty men across. And damned if they didn't
begin every one of their songs with the same word: *Girl.*

What is one thing you've inherited?

What stands out to you about the poem? What do you notice?

When you close your eyes, what visual images from the poem do you see? What words or phrases do you remember?

What do we learn from the title? What tone does it establish for the poem?

How do the first four words of the poem relate to the last four words?

Who is the "we" in this poem? Who is the "you?"

The poem is divided into two sections. How does this structure affect your understanding of the poem? Why is the poem divided there?

What dualities or oppositions do you see in the poem?

What proper nouns are used in the poem—noted through capitalization?

What does the poet accomplish by using alliteration (*repeated initial word sounds*) in the poem (*coupled, causing, confounded; feasted, familiar, fat*)? Are there other ways that sound contributes to the impact of the poem?

Read only the verbs in the poem. What, if anything, does this illuminate?

In what ways are inanimate objects and/or abstract concepts personified in this poem?

*Before workshop, print out copies of the worksheet for all participants to use in the exercise.*

*Read these instructions aloud to the workshop participants, giving them time to carry out each instruction before moving on to the next one.*

(1) Think of a time you felt different from the people around you in some way. What physical space are you in? Who else is there? Write down five concrete details about the physical space, and who else is in the space with you.

(2) Who are you in relation or opposition to these people? What defines you in this space (race, gender, class, age, clothing style, appetite, etc.)? Write down at least one and up to five things that define you in that space.

(3) In the first column of your worksheet, write a random noun or adjective. Pass it to your right.

(4) In the second column on the worksheet you've been handed, write a word the starts with the same sound as the word in the first column. Example: jungle—gym, or sweet—smart. Pass it to your right.

(5) In the third column, write a word that repeats some sound from the second column word. Example: gym—hymn, or smart—bar.

(6) Continue passing the worksheets around until all 10 columns are full. Fill them out quickly, without overthinking it.

(7) On the worksheet you receive with a completed chart, title your poem as a starting place using this format:

*A* _____ *(one of the defining characteristics from step 2) will* _____ *(verb/action) if you* _____ _____ *(verb/action).*

(8) Using this title as a springboard, freewrite using at least three of the phrases from the worksheet chart, as well as some of the details you noted in step 1 about the physical space and the people sharing that space with you.

| RANDOM NOUN OR ADJECTIVE | RANDOM NOUN OR ADJECTIVE | RANDOM NOUN OR ADJECTIVE |
|---|---|---|
| *jungle* | *gym* | *hymn* |
| *spiky* | *surplus* | *hug* |
| | | |
| | | |
| | | |
| | | |
| | | |
| | | |
| | | |
| | | |
| | | |
| | | |

A _____ (defining characteristic) will _____
_____ (verb/action) if you _____ (verb/action).

# MAN MATCHING DESCRIPTION

## *Jamaal May*

Because the silk scarf could have cradled
a neck as delicate as that of a cygnet,
but was instead used in last night's strangling,
it is possible to marvel at the finish on handcuffs.

Because I can imagine handcuffs,
pummeled by stones until shimmering,
the flashlight that sears my eyes
is too perfect to look away.

Because a flashlight has more power
on a southern roadside than my name and blood
combined and there is no power in the very human
frequency range of my voice and my name is dead
in my mouth and my name is in a clear font on a license
I can't reach for before being drawn down on—

Because the baton is long against my window,
the gun somehow longer against my cheek,
the vehicle cold against my abdomen
as my shirt rises, twisted in fingers
and my name is asked again—I want to
say, *Swan!* I am only a swan.

When have you been mistaken for someone else?

What stands out to you about the poem? What do you notice?

What is the impact of beginning each stanza in the poem with "because"? What other words or phrases are repeated in the poem?

Read just the last word of each line. Does this affect your understanding of the poem? How?

What role does sound play in this poem? How does the way words use repeating sounds like the S's in "because," "silk," and "scarf," or "drawn," "on," "baton," and "long" affect your reading and hearing of the poem? How does it relate to the poem's content?

What body parts are named in this poem? What other physical objects?

What visual images stand out to you in the poem? How do they contribute to your understanding of the poem?

What role does ambiguity (the sense of something possibly having more than one meaning) play in this poem?

What does the title tell us? How does it frame the poem? How does it connect to the last line?

What verbs stand out to you in this poem? How do they affect your reading of the poem?

What words or phrases give us context for this poem—geographic, temporal, etc.?

*Before the workshop, print out copies of the worksheet for all participants to use in the exercise.*

*Read these instructions aloud to the workshop participants, giving them time to carry out each instruction before moving on to the next one.*

(1) Take a worksheet and fill out ONLY the first column.

(2) Pass the worksheet to the person on your right.

(3) On the worksheet you have now, fill out the second column, so that it completes the sentence: When I hear the word _____, I think of _____. For example, when I hear the word SWAN, I think of INNOCENCE.

(4) On that same worksheet, write down a conjunction—because, without, unless, as if, although, after, before, neither, either, until, once, etc.

(5) Pass that worksheet to the right.

(6) Think of a time you wanted to say or do something but did not or could not. On the worksheet you have now, write down the thing you wanted to say or do but did not or could not.

(7) Using the word list on the worksheet you have now, and applying the qualities as directly or indirectly as you want, freewrite four stanzas each starting with the conjunction you were given. For example:

*Chicago / Violence. Unless Chicago tells me otherwise, I'll know cold as a thing that holds off the dying.*

(8) At some point in the poem, say or do the thing you wanted to say or do but did not or could not. Keep going, if you have time!

|  | ITEM | QUALITY PERTAINING TO IT |
|---|---|---|
| EXAMPLE: ANIMAL | *Swan* | *Innocence* |
| ANIMAL | | |
| ARTICLE OF CLOTHING | | |
| CITY | | |
| COMMON OBJECT | | |

A conjunction: _____

(*because, without, unless, as if, although, after, before, neither, either, until, once,* etc.)

Something you did not or could not say or do but wanted to:

# ALL HOOVES AND TEETH

## Jade Benoit

My body is no way to behave.

Last night, I fell asleep in my horse fur again
and I'm sorry. I know my habits are getting
out of hand but the animal sieved through me so deep
I even wore my fur out in the rain and shed a whole layer,
ruining all the kitchen towels. And that boy
is looking at me. Do you see him.
How he's looking. Like he knows about the bite marks
I keep leaving behind me, like he can see
my hooves trying to hold a dinner knife in old-time
cotillion fashion. And it's not that I'm a boy.  I swear
I'm not. It's just that, do you know what plucked fur
looks like floating loose in bath water.  Do you.
It's unnatural. So please don't look at my body
and what he's done to it.
It's fucked up. It's never functioned properly.
I'm all crosshatched, alternating white red grey
and my spine went pale from all the
*I'msorryNeverEverI'msorryPleaseDon't*
that tried to flee from my throat, instead
it grew so backwards and crowded inside me
that all I could do was hold on tight to his body
to make myself feel like I was still part
of the ground. Meanwhile, he just kept
painting and painting me in horse fur.
But Mother, you
are a thistle. Look at you.

I counted all the ways that I'm sorry
but they don't fall in sync with all the ways
you've shown me that Mother, I swear
to God you are the prettiest
and skinniest thing to rear its head
from this dirty old forest and
let me tell you something: there is a horse
inside me and all I want
is for that boy there to say, yes
that is the good stuff that is exactly
what I thought you would look like
under there.

What plant or flower reminds you of your mother?

## DISCUSSION QUESTIONS

What stands out to you about the poem? What do you notice?

Who is the "you" in this poem? How and when do we discover that, and how does it impact your reading/re-reading of the lines you read before discovering it?

The poem begins with a single line, then proceeds to a full stanza. How does this affect your understanding of the poem?

How does the title inform your reading of the poem?

When do the objects (hooves and teeth) from the title appear in the body of the poem? What actions do they take in the poem?

How are the interior and exterior worlds of the speaker contrasted and/or integrated in this poem?

What role does nature/the natural world play in this poem?

How would you describe the tone of this poem?

What do we learn about the speaker of the poem?

What role does looking play in the poem?

How is punctuation used in the poem?

# Exercise

*Read these instructions aloud to the workshop participants, giving them time to carry out each instruction before moving on to the next one.*

(1) List five characteristics of yourself (permanent or transitory):
*I am* _____

(2) Choose one of those characteristics, and write down its opposite:
*I am not* _____

(3) Who would want you to have this opposite characteristic? (For example, a priest would want me to be straight, my grandfather would want me to be rich, etc.)

(3) What animal represents that opposite characteristic? Write that down.

(4) List five characteristics of that animal.

(5) Freewrite a poem to the person who would want you to have that opposite characteristic, beginning with "My _____ is no _____." (Insert whatever words you like into the blanks. For example, "My body is no way to behave" or "My job is no flower garden.")

# THE HAPPY

*Ari Banias*

In a room more chicken coop than room,
I rent a fan that feels on my face like sound. Low traffic
from San Fernando, named for a king who
became a city, a valley, a saint.
We are meant to repeat his name. Instead
I say prickly pear, a cactus
which spreads its many-paddled hands
into the space around itself. No pears.
I call Mom to ask what the latest austerity measures mean.
Some ants on the wall make their way from one
unseeable point to another; the banks have closed.
I tell her to barter; barter what, she says.
An acquaintance posts "Tourism:
The Best Way to Be an Ally to Greece"
as if in each tourist's pleasure bloomed
a charity. Mules clabber down the stone paths
loaded with grapes to make next year's
wine, if the tourists come back
next year, and we hope they will. I say we,
but I'm closer to they. Living temporarily
in a neighborhood named for the happy, who were
who exactly?
I grow a little stiff with, a little lean with, a little faint with, a little
worn with seeming.
I must need to conquer my mind.
The roses dead because of drought
because whoever lives here cares enough
to let their roses die. I must

need to conquer the notion
anything needs conquering.
Something in me can't tell
what belongs. The ants
for whom anything is a street.
What sounded like a gate opening
was eucalyptus branches dragging themselves along the tin roof.
A yellow butterfly that has no interest in me.
I have no interest in kings.

What's something other people are obsessed with that you don't care about at all?

## DISCUSSION QUESTIONS

What stands out to you about the poem? What do you notice?

Where does this poem begin?

What actions does the "I" in the poem take?

Who speaks in the poem? What do they say, and to whom?

What is left ambiguous or unsaid in the poem? What is made specific?

What grows in this poem? What begins as one thing and becomes something else?

What is the role of permanence versus temporariness in this poem? What is permanent, and what is temporary?

Where do you see contradiction in this poem?

What repeats in the poem—what images, what words, what actions?

What is the role of geographic location in this poem?

How do the natural and human-made worlds interact in this poem?

How does the title affect your reading of the poem before you read it? Does reading the whole poem affect your understanding of the title?

*Before the workshop, print out copies of the worksheet.*

*Read these instructions aloud to the workshop participants, giving them time to carry out each instruction before moving on to the next one.*

(1) Complete the first three questions on your worksheet, without overthinking it. In all cases, write whatever comes to mind.

(2) Pass your completed worksheet to the right and fill in first column. Then, pass your worksheet to the right again and fill in second column. Then, hand back to the initial person.

(3) This worksheet is your word/idea bank. Freewrite a poem about that thing you have no interest in that so fascinates other people (from the introductory question) using whatever you can from the word/idea bank. Begin with the phrase "In a _____."

A country that is not the United States: _____

A family member: _____

A kind of insect: _____

For each of these words, write down the first word that comes to mind when you read it, then repeat for that word, continuing across the row:

| | | |
|---|---|---|
| clabber | | |
| austerity | | |
| eucalyptus | | |
| conquer | | |
| barter | | |
| drought | | |

# Dawn Lundy Martin

Almost every road leads to some dirt hole. One might have to pass a 15-room house, but there will be a dirt hole. There always is. Hole is a terrible word. If a child says, I put my finger down a hole, it sounds dirty. Dirty dirt hole. This is the first clue: avoid holes. If you can't, lie about it. Know what numbers know: their belonging. My parents' house in Connecticut is 314. My house now is 275. Three numbers are good. Three of anything is good. If there is a goodness in numbers, then there is a puzzle. Myopic vision alters the thing in front of the eyes. If holes are bad, then what am I? Are holes things with ends to them, or do they go on forever? One must decide. An aching toward a hole is an aching toward an invisibility. This is why it's difficult to be a girl. But, it's harder, much harder, to be the hole filler, the one who pushes up into an indefinable place, what's at the end of the road, and for sure, likened to something it is not, because no one knows what it is and there you are trying so desperately to do what you are supposed to do. I, too, am sick with worry. A shovel is in the hand. A cuff has bound the wrist. One thing is filled, another excavated. That's the trick. There is nothing in the world that is not exactly like this.

If you could choose one superpower to possess, what would it be?

What stands out to you about the poem? What do you notice?

What words repeat in the poem? What concepts?

How does the use of "one" instead of "you" as the second-person device affect your reading of the poem?

What words in the poem have to do with mystery?

If you had to choose one phrase or sentence as the heart of this poem, which would it be?

Does the poem begin with certainty or uncertainty? With which does it end?

What is the role of causation in the poem—if this, then this?

When you think about threes, what comes to mind? What are your connotations, connections with the number three?

What role do questions play in the poem? Is there a tension you could describe or name between the questions and the declarations?

How does the poet use passive and active voice throughout the poem?

How would this poem read differently if it were arranged with line breaks, rather than as a prose poem? How does its current configuration interact with its content?

*Before the workshop, print out copies of the worksheet for all participants to use in the exercise.*

Read these instructions aloud to the workshop participants, giving them time to carry out each instruction before moving on to the next one.

(1) List 12 aspects of your identity—things that you are, by choice or not. (Tall, a daughter, arthritic, thrifty, etc.)

(2) Circle the aspect of your identity that it is most difficult to be. Don't overthink it—positive things can also be difficult.

(3) Thinking of this aspect, write down:
- something related to nature
- a geographic location
- a number
- a tool
- a superpower that could also be a curse

(4) Keeping this aspect of your identity in mind, freewrite on or using the worksheet, filling in the blanks. Incorporate the list of items you just brainstormed whenever you get stuck.

Almost every _____

_____

One might _____

_____

There always _____

_____

_____ is a terrible _____

_____

If a _____

_____

This is the first _____

_____

If you _____

_____

_____ Know _____

My _____

_____

My _____

_____

_____ are good. _____

_____

_____ is good. If there _____

_____

the thing in front _____

_____

If _____

_____

Are _____

_____

One must _____

_____

_____ toward a _____

This is why _____

_____

But, it's _____

_____

_____ because no one _____

_____

I, too, am _____

_____

A _____

_____

A _____

_____

One thing _____

_____

That's the _____

_____

There is _____

# TORSO OF A WOMAN

## Allison Benis White

Like touching her without fingers, then having fingers, the discharge of electricity may take place between one part of a cloud and another, one cloud and another, a cloud and the earth. In the postcard, lightning is three-pronged above a single house, like a fork sinking into a piece of white cake. Being touched without warning, a person is likely to jump or make an animal-like noise, unfamiliar as your own recorded voice, but the house stays still. Inside one bedroom, a child might wake to lightning and think of her legs under the covers for reasons she doesn't immediately understand. I am interested in suddenness.

If there is no way to prepare, then there is nothing to worry about. But if you think about the hundreds of possible outcomes, it sounds like a truck crashing through the roof. Listening awake, I will hold my body as still as possible. Doing nothing is an action. Prayer is an action. The house I grew up in has the same iron address numbers nailed to a rectangular board, but the new owner wouldn't let me or my father in. Because we were over. Because, in the big picture, we own nothing. Afraid at night, when you enter someone else's room, it is important to whisper her name before you touch her, so she knows you are approaching, and does not become alarmed.

Thunder is louder than a human voice could ever protest, and without a pattern. There's no way to be sure. In 1939, after *The Wizard of Oz* was released, seventeen girls ran from their homes, open-armed, into tornadoes and died. I suppose it was just a way to feel certain, to encounter, violently, the verge of relief, just as, in a storm, the front door rips off at the rusted hinges, no longer separating the house from the earth. Without a door, it is not your house. Without a house, the children are not sane. I'd wait for the whine of the garage door at night, a broken man's whine, my father's warm, humming bones, then reversed, like the sky coming down. If only the rain would ease into sleep with me, soak through and be finished, I could breathe.

What movie do you most vividly remember seeing? (Can be recent or long past.)

What stands out to you about the poem? What do you notice?

What do you make of the title? Why "torso"? How would it be different with a different body part, or a more specific description than "a woman" (name or adjective included)? What does the use of "woman" rather than "girl" in the title indicate to you?

What kind of sentence starts each stanza? What does that do to you as the reader? What follows in each?

What would you say is the underlying central desire in this poem? What does the speaker most want?

Circle all the phrases that start with *I* or *we*—what sub-story does that tell? How does this relate, if at all, to the rest of the poem?

Who gets touched in the poem, and by whom? How? What is the significance of the touching? What happens with regard to touching in the last stanza?

What images of containment do you see in the poem? Release? What does the containing? What does the releasing? What is contained? What is released? How does this relate, if at all, to the last line of the poem?

What kinds of sentences are used, in what order, to what affect? (Long versus short, simple versus complex, etc.)

What, if anything, links the stanzas to each other across the breaks? What impact do the stanza breaks have on you as a reader? How would the poem be different without them, or with additional ones?

Does the act of touching her *create* fingers, or does "then" just imply the passage of time?

What is the role of the storm in the poem? What kind of storms are included/alluded to? What is the impact of the *Wizard of Oz* reference?

How do thought and meaning move, one sentence to the next?

*Before the workshop, lay out five bowls labeled movie, dessert, building, year, and weather. Cut enough slips of paper that each participant gets five.*

*Read these instructions aloud to the workshop participants, giving them time to carry out each instruction before moving on to the next one.*

(1) You have five slips of paper. Please write on the first, a movie title. Put it in the bowl marked "movie." On the second, a dessert. Put that in the "dessert" bowl. Repeat with a physical structure/building. Next, a year. Finally, a word having to do with weather.

(2) Quickly, without thinking too hard, write down five things you want.

(3) Circle one of those things.

(3) What is behind that desire? For example, you want a job. Behind that is the desire for money. Write down that desire.

(4) Now, what is behind THAT desire? For example, behind the desire for money is the desire for stability.

(5) Repeat one more time.

(6) Write down a childhood memory, whatever comes to mind right now.

(7) Pull one piece of paper from each bowl.

Starting with "Like" and one of the words pulled from the bowls, freewrite about that final desire. Integrate the memory and the other words/concepts from the bowls.

# ODE TO SLEEPING IN MY CLOTHES

*Ross Gay*

And though I don't mention it
to my mother
or the doctors
with their white coats
it is, in fact,
a great source of happiness,
for me, as I don't
even remove my socks,
and will sometimes
even pull up my hood
and slide my hands deep
in my pockets
and probably moreso
than usual look as if something
bad has happened
my heart blasting a last somersault
or some artery parting
like curtains in a theatre
while the cavalry of blood
comes charging through
except unlike
so many of the dead
I must be smiling
there in my denim
and cotton sarcophagus
slightly rank from the day
it is said that Shostakovich slept
with a packed suitcase beneath

his bed and it is said
that black people were snatched
from dark streets and made experiments
of and you and I
both have family whose life
savings are tucked 12 feet beneath
the Norway maple whose roots
splay like the bones
in the foot of man
who has walked to Youngstown, Ohio
from Mississippi without sleeping
or keeping his name
and it's a miracle
maybe I almost never think of
to rise like this
and simply by sliding my feet into my boots
while the water for coffee
gathers its song
be in the garden
or on the stoop
running, almost,
from nothing.

What is the weirdest thing you love to do? (For example, eating cottage cheese with seasoning salt, plucking arm hairs, taking cold baths, etc.)

## DISCUSSION QUESTIONS

What stands out to you about the poem? What do you notice?

Who are the characters in this poem? What do we learn about each?

How would you describe the tone or overall feeling of this poem?

What do you notice about the use of punctuation in the poem? How does that affect your reading of it?

What is the role of refusal in this poem?

What is named in this poem? Where else does the subject of naming arise?

Who, aside from the speaker, sleeps in this poem?

What actions are taken in the poem, by the speaker or other people or objects? What actions are not taken?

What sounds do you hear repeated in the poem? How does that affect you as a reader/listener?

Does the poem ever turn or pivot from its original direction? If so, in what direction does it turn?

What do you make of the speaker's comparison of his sleeping self to a corpse?

## Exercise

*Read these instructions aloud to the workshop participants, giving them time to carry out each instruction before moving on to the next one.*

(1) Picture yourself doing that weird thing you love to do. Close your eyes and imagine it in as much detail as you can. Where are you? Who else is there? What do you smell, taste, hear, see? What are you feeling?

(2) I'm going to ask you a series of questions. Thinking of what you just pictured, answer each in a full sentence. Just write whatever comes to mind without worrying about logic or being right. For example, if I ask, "What do you taste?" you might write down "I taste red salt and old milk" or "What I taste is the moon," or even "I don't taste anything."

- Where are you?
- What do you smell?
- Who would be surprised that you love this thing?
- Does what you love love you back? How do you know?
- Who or what do you look like in this moment?
- What do you do after you do this thing?
- What could make you stop doing it?

(3) Choose one of these sentences as the first line of your poem. Freewrite from there, using the other sentences in whatever order you like, writing between them to create your draft.

# PLAY IT AGAIN

*Ada Limón*

Up above a bar in their first apartment,
my ma and my dad are in some whorl
of late '60s haze in the Castro District
of San Francisco where the jukebox
below played the same Frankie Valli song,
*Sherry, Sherry baby, Sherry, Sherry baby*
until they go almost mad with their
paper floors and cheap wall hangings
swinging in the falsetto of the city's
changing swirl of hips and hopes
and I love them so. She's in the window
crying because the city is too big, and also
because we are at war, and he goes to work
in hard schools that need teachers,
Spanish-speaking teachers not scared of much
except how to make rent and make the world maybe
better or easier or livable. Nights, they get stoned
in small apartments and eat enchiladas
in the warm corn-filled kitchens
and she's going to paint and have big ideas,
and he's going to save the world with curriculum,
and no one knew how much that want matters,
how much the ordinary need to make some real life
was enough to give them the drive to make
some real nice mistakes. How years later,
some might say that their love was not a love,
or was not the right kind of love, but rather
a sort of holding on in order to escape another

trapped fate of desert heat and parental push,
but I want to tell you, nothing was an accident.
Not their innocence or their ideals, not their
selfish need, not their dark immortal laughter,
not the small place with the roaring traffic, not
the bus rides, or riots, or carelessness and calm,
not the world that wanted them in it, that needed
their small, young faces united in kiss and weep,
not the song that surrounded them in a good fight,
that repeated, *Come, come, come out tonight.*

What song reminds you of your family?

What stands out to you about the poem? What do you notice?

How many sentences does this poem have? How does the length of those sentences and their consistency or inconsistency affect your reading of the poem?

What details stand out to you in the poem?

What is affirmed in this poem? What is negated or refused?

How does the title relate to the poem overall, particularly its ending?

What is the role of repetition in this poem?

Who are the characters in this poem? What do we learn about them?

How is this poem's historical moment and context established? How does it affect your reading of the poem?

What is declared in this poem, and to whom?

What happens with time in this poem? What is known, and what is conjectured?

Which of the five senses are invoked in this poem, and how?

*Read these instructions aloud to the workshop participants, giving them time to carry out each instruction before moving on to the next one.*

(1) Think of a story about one or more members of your family. This story can be true or mythical or entirely invented.

(2) Pair up with another workshop participant and tell that story in as much detail as you can within two minutes. If you can't remember details or facts, make them up. Listeners, listen intently but *do not* take notes.

(3) Listeners, tell that story back to the person who told it originally. Change whatever details you like, accidentally because you can't remember them, or on purpose just to change the story.

(4) Reverse roles—listener becomes storyteller, and vice versa. Repeat the process of telling and telling back.

(5) Freewrite that story as a poem, using whatever true or invented "facts" you like, those from the original story, those you came up with, and/or those invented by your partner.

Start by mentioning a physical location and incorporate at least two of the five senses (smell, touch, taste, hearing, and sight).

# PEOPLE, THE GHOSTS DOWN IN NORTH-OF-THE-SOUTH AREN'T SEE-THROUGH

## *Diane Seuss*

They don't wear nightgowns or whisper or sing
or want hazy things from the ones of us who are living.
They have skin, bones, people. They're short in stature
and they don't walk through walls. They come in our houses

by kicking down doors, wearing porkpie hats and smoking
those My Father cigars. Yellow sweat stains
on their sleeveless undershirts, my people. I'm sure
there are other kinds of ghosts other places,

sad angels wearing bloomers and fanning their wings,
but here their faces are made of gristle and their eyes
red from too much Thunderbird. They want to steal
our valuables, mess shit up, drop a match and burn

down the house. I don't know any other way to say it,
people. They walk right into our kitchens without being invited,
tracking mud, lifting the fish by the tail out of the fryer
and stuffing it in a cloth sack the color of a potato

just pulled out of the ground, and if there was a potato
pulled fresh out of the ground they'd take that too.
Their pee sizzles when it hits the floor. They don't hear
prayers or heed four-leaf clovers. We have to give

our bodies to the task. I mean we push back, people.
Harder than day labor. Harder than shoving a bull
out of the cow paddock. Two bulls. We have to say
leave my goddamned house. Go, motherfucker.

My fucking house. Shouting while pushing, like breach birth,
or twins. They slap on that corpse-smelling aftershave
and come calling, holding a bouquet of weeds. They want
our whiskey, our gravy, our honey, our combs, our bees.

INTRODUCTORY QUESTION

What is something most people don't know about the place you come from?

DISCUSSION QUESTIONS

What stands out to you about the poem? What do you notice?

How does the title bring you into the poem as a reader? How would you describe the tone of the title?

What do you make of the repeated term "people"?

Who are the groups of characters in this poem? Who are the "we," who are the "they"? To whom is the poem directed?

What details stand out to you in the poem?

How would you describe the speaker's voice in this poem?

How does the poet use sentence structure—fragments, simple sentences, stacks of clauses—in the poem?

Read just the first two words in each sentence of the poem. Does this affect your reading or understanding of the poem in any way?

Why would a ghost wear "corpse-smelling aftershave"? What would this accomplish?

If the ghosts in this poem were not actual ghosts, what or who might they be? Would this affect your interpretation of who the "we" in the poem represents?

How is enjambment—continuing a sentence across a line or stanza break—used in this poem?

How are the items listed in the final sentence of the poem related to each other, and to the rest of the poem?

*Read these instructions aloud to the workshop participants, giving them time to carry out each instruction before moving on to the next one.*

(1) Think about where you come from, however you define that. Close your eyes and picture it.

(2) What ghosts haunt that place, literally or metaphorically? Answer these questions about them, just writing whatever comes to mind:

- What do they wear?
- What do they listen to on the radio?
- What do they eat?
- How do they get into buildings or homes?
- What do they do when they get inside?
- Where do they like to go most?
- What do they drink?
- What do they love?
- What do they want?

(3) Drawing on the answers to those questions, write something directed to a person or group of people unlikely to understand the place you come from, and its ghosts. If it helps, start with "They don't ..."

# DEATH: BARON SAMEDI

*Kwame Dawes*

First your dog dies and you pray
for the Holy Spirit to raise the inept
lump in the sack, but Jesus' name
is no magic charm; sunsets and the
flies are gathering. That is how faith
dies. By dawn you know death;
the way it arrives and then grows
silent. Death wins. So you walk
out to the tangle of thorny weeds behind
the barn; and you coax a black
cat to your fingers. You let it lick
milk and spit from your hand before
you squeeze its neck until it messes
itself, it claws tearing your skin,
its eyes growing into saucers.
A dead cat is light as a live
one and not stiff, not yet. You
grab its tail and fling it as
far as you can. The crows find
it first; by then the stench
of the hog pens hides the canker
of death. Now you know the power
of death, that you have it,
that you can take life in a second
and wake the same the next day.
This is why you can't fear death.
You have seen the broken neck
of a man in a well, you know who

pushed him over the lip of the well,
tumbling down; you know all about
blood on the ground. You know that
a dead dog is a dead cat is a dead
man. Now you look a white man
in the face, talk to him about
cotton prices and the cost of land,
laugh your wide open mouthed laugh
in his face, and he knows one thing
about you: that you know the power
of death, and you will die as easily
as live. This is how a man seizes
what he wants, how a man
turns the world over in dreams,
eats a solid meal and waits
for death to come like nothing,
like the open sky, like light
at early morning. Like a man
in a red pin striped trousers, a black
top hat, a yellow scarf
and a kerchief dipped in eau
de cologne to cut through
the stench coming from his mouth.

What was your first pet?

What stands out to you about the poem? What do you notice?

What role does time play in the poem, specifically related to the order of things (first, then, etc.)?

How does the poet address *causality*—if this, then this?

How does knowledge about the "you" in the poem arrive? What do we learn about this "you" and when do we learn those things?

Look at how the sentences in the poem are structured—are they consistent or inconsistent in their structure? Are they simple or complex?

Are there any lines in the poem that contain only one sentence—where a sentence is not enjambed (broken) across the line break?

What is the longest sentence in the poem? What is the shortest sentence in the poem?

Do we ever learn the race of the "you" in the poem? Is it significant?

Do we ever learn the gender of the "you" in the poem? Is it significant?

How many times is the word *death* or variations on it used in the poem? How many times is the word *life* or variations on it used?

*This is why you can't fear death.* Does this read to you as "you are unable to fear death" or "you should not/must not fear death"—or both? Or neither?

What colors are mentioned in the poem? When? What significance might this have?

Who is named in the poem?

What line feels like the heart or center of the poem to you?

Does anything in the poem surprise you? If so, what?

*Before workshop, write enough big vague concepts on slips of paper that everyone in the workshop can select at least one. Example: death, war, sorrow, poverty, envy, etc. Fold these and put them in a bowl so that each participants can draw one without knowing what it is.*

*Print out copies of the worksheet for all participants to use in the exercise.*

*Read these instructions aloud to the workshop participants, giving them time to carry out each instruction before moving on to the next one.*

(1) Choose a big vague concept from the bowl.

(2) Invent a minor god, deity or demon in charge of this, and write out their characteristics on your worksheet.

(3) Use the structure below that on the worksheet to start your freewrite. Fill in the blanks with as much language as you like, and go from there.

# Worksheet

CONCEPT: _____

Gender: _____

Article of clothing: _____

Drink of choice: _____

Preferred time of day: _____

Two-word sentence: _____
                     (concept) (i.e., "Death")

_____.
     (verb) (i.e., "wins.")

*Use this structure to start your poem:*


First


then


By _____
        (time of day)


_____     _____.

        (Two-word sentence).


So

# ROOM LIT BY A BULLET &
# A PHOTOGRAPH OF A PONY

*Nina Puro*

What you did was a bullet, but I've drilled a hole through it
         & wear it around my neck. Sure you got a key—I've seen it—
but it's a cheap one from the mall like every other crush has:
         plating wearing to brass. It don't open any locks.
In this Western, I ride bareback. Once I peed in the holy water &
         saw graves yawn open to flowers. When daddy said drown kittens I did
& didn't cry. Today, I'm double-fisting anything I can &
         waiting for the river to become a cracked riverbed I can walk along
towards the scaffold I'm waiting to finish building. There's solitude
         in the long warm furrows of dirt in fields & in standing at the front
of a crowded train looking down the tunnel; a question
         about loneliness in the long barrels of pistols. (In a cold shovelful
of dirt hitting wood lined with fake satin, slow like how a balloon sinks
         slower in a dirty room.) An answer to the question in using favorite forks
& breaking favorite plates & in lightning bugs trapped in jars.

What you were: a photograph of a horse to someone
         who's never been on a horse. What I am: hordes of kids riding bareback
off cliffs with satin ribbons in their hair & the horses' manes,
         the satin trailing up to form a picture that shows where they're going next.
I had the same dream seventeen times in a row & I had it because I slept alone
         for once. Solitude in lipstick: a weapon by the bed brightening
as the cigarettes in the ashtray & the fireflies nod
         out; solitude as the long black car arrives & the door clicks shut
with the sound of a phone cord being cut. (There's the end of
         solitude in the mirror on the ceiling. In the knock. In waking up
thirsty & drinking cold water.) Falling back asleep

to have the dream an eighteenth time, only this time all the faces are blurs
but I know who everyone is. (This time we're all dead.)

Every person's voice is still ice clinking in a glass, but now
everything costs $5.99: almost a dollar more than I've got.


We depart, go new places—there's dust in our hair
        & not enough air in our lungs to blow the balloon back up.
I couldn't taste the metal in your key because of the glue on my tongue.

        If you chew gum while you dissect cadavers, it'll taste of formaldehyde.
I can taste my death in stamps & almonds (& if I spit the bitterness
        into the trashcan, I won't absorb it, but if I hold it on my tongue,
it turns sweet). I've been places downriver you aren't allowed
        to have shoelaces or listen to music or be alone. Where someone
sits in a chair & watches you sleep. When you sleep, sometimes you move
        through the dark. Sometimes the dark moves through you. Sometimes
the dark asks questions; sometimes it shoots.

When do you remember being angry as a child?

What stands out to you about the poem? What do you notice?

What repeats in this poem—what images, ideas, objects? What is the impact of that repetition?

How would this poem be different if the stanzas appeared in a different order?

In what kind of place are you not allowed to have shoelaces, listen to music, or be alone? How does the fact that the speaker has been in this kind of place inform your reading of the poem?

What do we learn about the "you" in this poem? Must it necessarily be a person?

What is the role of time in this poem?

What references to physical movement do you see in the poem? How do these connect or relate to each other and/or to the poem as a whole?

How does each sentence of the poem begin? How does the ordinariness of that scaffold affect your ability to read the poem, to absorb the images and ideas it contains?

Which of the five senses are engaged in this poem? How?

What does the use of "sometimes" in the last few lines imply to you?

What do you make of the title? How is it connected to the poem's ending?

*Before the workshop, cut enough slips of paper for each participant to receive nine. Also print out copies of the worksheet with the starter phrases so that each participant can have one.*

*Distribute the slips of paper so that each participant has nine. Read these instructions aloud to the workshop participants, giving them time to carry out each instruction before moving on to the next one.*

(1) You have nine pieces of paper. Please write on the first slip: an animal. On the second: a tool. Next slip: a weapon. Then on the other slips (one per slip): a body of water, a kind of fabric, a vehicle, a body part, a kind of insect, and a household item. Pass all the slips in to me.

(2) List five people who have made you incredibly angry—it doesn't have to be someone you know personally, but it can be. This can be recent or long past, doesn't matter.

(3) Circle one of those people.

(4) Look at the list of starter phrases on your worksheet. Starting with one of these phrases, freewrite a poem speaking to a "you"—the person you circled who angered or angers you. Use the starter phrases as jumping-off points for the following sentences, to keep writing and build momentum. You can go in order, but don't have to.

Every minute or two, I will come around and hand you one of these slips of paper. Use this word either in the sentence you're writing at that time or the following one. Don't worry about making logical sense—follow where the process takes you and leave logic to the revision stage.

# Worksheet

Starter phrases:

*What you did*

*And sure*

*It doesn't*

*In this*

*Once I*

*When*

*Today, I'm*

*There is*

*In a*

*An answer to*

*What you were: a*

*What I am:*

*I had the*

# PRAYER

*Keetje Kuipers*

Perhaps as a child you had the chicken pox
and your mother, to soothe you in your fever
or to help you fall asleep, came into your room
and read to you from some favorite book,
*Charlotte's Web* or *Little House on the Prairie*,
a long story that she quietly took you through
until your eyes became magnets for your shuttering
lids and she saw your breathing go slow. And then
she read on, this time silently and to herself,
not because she didn't know the story,
it seemed to her that there had never been a time
when she didn't know this story—the young girl
and her benevolence, the young girl in her sod house—
but because she did not yet want to leave your side
though she knew there was nothing more
she could do for you. And you, not asleep but simply weak,
listened to her turn the pages, still feeling
the lamp warm against one cheek, knowing the shape
of the rocking chair's shadow as it slid across
your chest. So that now, these many years later,
when you are clenched in the damp fist of a hospital bed,
or signing the papers that say you won't love him anymore,
when you are bent at your son's gravesite or haunted
by a war that makes you wake with the gun
cocked in your hand, you would like to believe
that such generosity comes from God, too,

who now, when you have the strength to ask, might begin
the story again, just as your mother would,
from the place where you have both left off.

What book have you not read, but always meant to read?

What stands out to you about the poem? What do you notice?

How does starting the poem with "perhaps" impact your reading of it?

How many sentences are there in this poem? How does the sentence structure affect your reading of it?

How does this poem being in second person—directed to a "you"— affect your reading of it? How would it be different if it were written in first person?

When does the poem's location change, and how?

How does time work in the poem? Is it linear, cyclical, or something else?

What visual images stand out to you in the poem?

Would the poem feel different if there were stanza breaks? How so?

Which of the five senses (smell, touch, taste, hearing, sight) are engaged in this poem? How?

What role does ambiguity—things not being exact or precisely laid out—play in the poem? What is exact, and what is ambiguous?

How are the title and the last line related to one another?

*Have blank paper and pens available for each participant.*

*Read these instructions aloud to the workshop participants, giving them time to carry out each instruction before moving on to the next one.*

(1) On your paper, write down:

- a book title
- a cause of suffering
- a piece of furniture
- a source of relief
- a positive attribute (generosity, kindness, etc.)
- an increment of time (day, decade, minute, etc.)

(2) Pass your paper with these notes to the right.

(3) Think of a time you've been comforted by someone. Doesn't have to be an epic moment—any example will do.

(4) Keeping the feeling of that comfort in mind, tell a different story, the story of someone being relieved of the suffering indicated on the paper you were handed, by the source written there. Incorporate the book title, the furniture, and the positive attribute. If possible, move around in the increment of time indicated. Start with "Perhaps," if it's helpful.

# ALABANZA: IN PRAISE OF LOCAL 100

*for the 43 members of Hotel Employees and Restaurant Employees*
*Local 100, working at the Windows on the World restaurant,*
*who lost their lives in the attack on the World Trade Center*

## Martín Espada

*Alabanza.* Praise the cook with a shaven head
and a tattoo on his shoulder that said *Oye,*
a blue-eyed Puerto Rican with people from Fajardo,
the harbor of pirates centuries ago.
Praise the lighthouse in Fajardo, candle
glimmering white to worship the dark saint of the sea.
*Alabanza.* Praise the cook's yellow Pirates cap
worn in the name of Roberto Clemente, his plane
that flamed into the ocean loaded with cans for Nicaragua,
for all the mouths chewing the ash of earthquakes.
*Alabanza.* Praise the kitchen radio, dial clicked
even before the dial on the oven, so that music and Spanish
rose before bread. Praise the bread. *Alabanza.*

Praise Manhattan from a hundred and seven flights up,
like Atlantis glimpsed through the windows of an ancient aquarium.
Praise the great windows where immigrants from the kitchen
could squint and almost see their world, hear the chant of nations:
*Ecuador, México, Republica Dominicana,*
*Haiti, Yemen, Ghana, Bangladesh.*
*Alabanza.* Praise the kitchen in the morning,
where the gas burned blue on every stove
and exhaust fans fired their diminutive propellers,
hands cracked eggs with quick thumbs
or sliced open cartons to build an altar of cans.

*Alabanza.* Praise the busboy's music, the chime-chime
of his dishes and silverware in the tub.
*Alabanza.* Praise the dish-dog, the dishwasher
who worked that morning because another dishwasher
could not stop coughing, or because he needed overtime
to pile the sacks of rice and beans for a family
floating away on some Caribbean island plagued by frogs.

*Alabanza.* Praise the waitress who heard the radio in the kitchen
and sang to herself about a man gone. *Alabanza.*

After the thunder wilder than thunder,
after the shudder deep in the glass of the great windows,
after the radio stopped singing like a tree full of terrified frogs,
after night burst the dam of day and flooded the kitchen,
for a time the stoves glowed in darkness like the lighthouse in Fajardo,
like a cook's soul. Soul I say, even if the dead cannot tell us
about the bristles of God's beard because God has no face,
soul I say, to name the smoke-beings flung in constellations
across the night sky of this city and cities to come.
*Alabanza* I say, even if God has no face.

*Alabanza.* When the war began, from Manhattan and Kabul
two constellations of smoke rose and drifted to each other,
mingling in icy air, and one said with an Afghan tongue:
*Teach me to dance. We have no music here.*
And the other said with a Spanish tongue:
*I will teach you. Music is all we have.*

What have you always wanted to write about but haven't?
(This can be anything! As big and heavy as "nuclear war" to as specific and personal as "the way my grandmother baked bread.")

DISCUSSION QUESTIONS

What stands out to you about the poem? What do you notice?

How is sound used in the poem—both the sounds of words and what is heard or spoken?

What do you notice about body parts in this poem?

Who are the characters in this poem? What do we learn about them?

What is the role of geographic location in the poem? Where do we begin, where do we go, where do we end?

What words and concepts repeat in this poem? What is the impact of this repetition?

What pattern is established in the poem's structure? Where does this pattern change? Does this reflect a change in content or perspective as well?

How does the speaker in this poem establish authenticity or believability?

How would you describe the tone of this poem?

How does this poem handle the progression of time, and events in time?

What do you notice about the length and structure of the stanzas? How does this reflect or create friction with the poem's content?

When does the "I" enter the poem? What does the "I" do? What do you make of this timing?

# Exercise

*Read these instructions aloud to the workshop participants, giving them time to carry out each instruction before moving on to the next one.*

(1) Think about that topic or experience you've always wanted to write about but not been able to. Answer these questions as quickly as you can.

- What building is that topic or experience?
- What animal is that topic or experience?
- What country is that topic or experience?
- What is the central emotion you feel when you think about this?
- What is behind or underneath that emotion?
- What is behind or underneath THAT emotion?
- Close your eyes and visualize it as a snapshot. Who is in the photo?
- Who is just outside the frame of the photo?
- Who knows way more about this than you do? (Can be an individual or a group of people.)
- Who makes you feel something strongly about this topic or experience? (Can be an individual or a group of people.)

(2) Choose one of the people from the last few questions. You'll write your poem to or about them.

(3) Decide whether you want to write a praise poem or a curse poem.

(4) Drawing from the list of information you created through the questions, freewrite about or to your selected person or group of people. Start by praising or cursing one, and giving us some detail about them.

# SHE CONSIDERS TRADING HER SECRETS

## Catherine Pierce

These girls, she says. These girls, I could smite them.
These girls, if they knew about the tree inside me, or

the rabbit trap, or the plastic doll parts. If they knew
about the dog I walk each night in my dreams, her big

teeth showing, her paws like dinner plates. If they knew
how I like knowing she could eat me but chooses not to.

That is how I feel safest. These girls. If they saw me lit
by the dome light of my station wagon. If they saw me under

his hands during the ice storm. What would they say?
Would they kiss me? Would they share their licorice

and chlamydia? Would we talk about equations as if
they held the world? Oh, these girls. They are dumb

as bicycles. Their eyes like tree knots. Their smiles
like paper. If they knew that my world is not their world,

is gloaming-colored and damp, echoes with howls and bells,
floats in the space between the desert and the past—

would they ride the carousel next to me? Would they,
for once, give me the best horse?

Where or among whom do you feel the greatest sense of belonging?

What stands out to you about the poem? What do you notice?

What do you make of the word "smite" in the first line? What does that word bring to mind? Who or what smites people?

What three things are inside the "she"? (Tree, rabbit trap, plastic doll parts, etc.) What do these things tell us? How are they related to each other?

What do we learn about the character referred to as "she" in the poem?

What do we learn about "these girls"?

Are there any other characters in the poem? What do we learn about them?

What role does repetition play in the poem?

Let's hear someone read just the first three words of each sentence aloud. What does that do to our understanding of the poem?

Let's hear someone read just the first word of each sentence aloud. What does that do to our understanding of the poem?

What animals are mentioned in the poem? What does each bring to mind for you?

What do you make of the dog? What do we learn about the dog?

What is the function of similes (for example, "paws like dinner plates") in this poem?

What is the role of uncertainty in the poem? What is the role of the hypothetical?

What do we learn from the title? What can we conjecture from it? What does it mean to consider trading secrets?

Why do these girls have the power to give her the best horse on the carousel? What is the relationship or power dynamic between "them" and "she"?

*Read these instructions aloud to the workshop participants, giving them time to carry out each instruction before moving on to the next one.*

(1) Think of the last dream you can remember. If you're comfortable doing so, close your eyes and picture it. If you're not comfortable closing your eyes, just look down at the floor.

(2) If your eyes were closed, open them and write down six details from that dream memory—words or phrases, images, characters, sensations, etc.

(3) Think about a time in your life when you felt like an outsider. It could be passing through an unfamiliar neighborhood, at a family reunion, in an expensive restaurant or store, meeting a significant other's family—whatever first comes to mind.

If you're comfortable doing so, close your eyes and picture it. If you're not comfortable closing your eyes, just look down at the floor. Picture this moment in as much detail as you can. Who else is there? Where are you? What are the sounds? Smells? Open your eyes and make a few notes about what you saw.

(4) I'm going to give you some jumping-off points, and about a minute to freewrite based on each. Don't overthink these, just write down whatever comes to mind until I give the next prompt. Don't worry about it making sense or being "poetic."

(5) Look at that list of details from your dream. Describe something that happened or something you saw.

(6) Look at your notes about the time you felt like an outsider. Describe something you saw, heard, smelled, or tasted.

(7) A character from the dream enters (could be you or someone else). What do they do?

(8) Write something a person said or something else you heard when you felt like an outsider.

(9) Continue freewriting, integrating elements of the dream situation and the outsider situation without worrying about making logical sense.

# WAKE UP YOUR SAINTS AND
# SETTLE DOWN FOR THE NIGHT

## Sasha Fletcher

I pull a raised platform strung up with lights out of my mouth
without much difficulty and then I stand on the stage and wait
while a crowd gathers. What are you doing they say
and I tell them that I am performing miracles.
I start by placing all of their trouble in my mouth
until the world seems brighter
and this brightness is directly related
to the lights on my stage. I receive wild
and unheralded applause. At the edge of town
is a vast encroaching darkness.
Can you swallow that too they say
and I tell them I can swallow that too. Soon after
I retire. I build a house in the country
and read many books on gardening and sunsets.
Every day I awake at dawn and take my coffee and bask
in my seclusion. There are tulips on the table
but I remain dissatisfied.
I raise up an army of the dead and gather them in the woods.
We prepare to march on the town. My army of the dead
does not ask questions and I like that about them.
We are getting excited. We are practicing our dance routines
and death by defenestration. We are oiling up our guns
and tying together our limbs. Pretty soon
it's a real horror show out here. My army of the dead
takes offense at the term Horror Show. I do not tolerate insubordination
and so I bury them in the ground. After that

I throw sheets over everything in my house.

I tell the townspeople that these are all ghosts.

They ask me what I am planning on doing about these ghosts.

I tell them nothing.

What is your favorite fairytale?

What stands out to you about the poem? What do you notice?

What is given in the poem, and what is received? What is consumed, and what is produced?

How does the poem being written in present tense affect your reading of it? How would it be different if it were in past tense?

What is spoken/said in the poem, and by whom?

What do you make of the poem's title?

What is the role of chronological time in the poem?

What in the poem occurs in nature? What is human-built/human-made?

What happens in town? What happens outside of it?

Read just the last word of each line. Does this affect your understanding of the poem in any way?

How would it affect your reading of the poem if it were divided into stanzas? How does the single-stanza format affect your understanding of the poem, and reflect or create tension with its content?

What physical actions does the "I" in the poem take?

How do you interpret the last line of this poem? Are there other lines that could have multiple interpretations?

*Before the workshop, print out copies of the worksheet for all participants to use in the exercise.*

*Read these instructions aloud to the workshop participants, giving them time to carry out each instruction before moving on to the next one.*

(1) Think of a story you don't want to tell, or haven't been able to tell. Make a note of it on your worksheet.

(2) Complete the first column on the worksheet—who are the characters involved in your story? Where does it take place? What objects are present and/or involved?

(3) Choose either a zoo or a garden as the overall symbol for the world of your poem. Complete the second column on the worksheet with this in mind. See the example for guidance.

(4) Once you've completed the worksheet, freewrite your poem using the information from the second column—retelling the story but substituting the allegorical/metaphorical characters, location, objects and anything else relevant. Think of this as code, or symbols, if that's helpful.

Begin with an action taken by you or someone else in the story.

*A story you don't want to tell or haven't been able to tell:*

**CHARACTERS:**

| Actual | Zoo or garden version |
|---|---|
|  |  |
|  |  |
|  |  |
|  |  |
|  |  |

**LOCATION:**

| Actual | Zoo or garden version |
|---|---|
|  |  |

**IMPORTANT OBJECTS:**

| Actual | Zoo or garden version |
|---|---|
|  |  |
|  |  |
|  |  |
|  |  |

*Retell the story, replacing the actual with the metaphorical/allegorical.*

**EXAMPLE:** Sitting by grandma's bed alone, days before she died.

**CHARACTERS:**

| Actual | Zoo or garden version |
|---|---|
| Myself | Gardener |
| Grandma | Rose bush |
|  |  |
|  |  |
|  |  |

**LOCATION:**

| Actual | Zoo or garden version |
|---|---|
| Hospice room | Corner of the garden, by the wall |

**IMPORTANT OBJECTS:**

| Actual | Zoo or garden version |
|---|---|
| Hospital bed | Patch of garden soil |
| Television | Noisy bugs—bees! |
| Bible | Gardening manual |
|  |  |

# WEIGHT

*Rachel McKibbens*

He interrupted winter with his own.
Over chocolate cake & Jimmy Stewart
I got the news. Couldn't stay

on the phone long, no room
left in me for the shaming
language: *Stupid. Selfish. Waste.*

Over time it became *the accident*—
too drunk to count all the pills
he'd taken. No need to discuss
the tragedies of lineage.

What was in the blood stayed.
His fanged veins, shot liver
& all that dark honey chalked up
to shit arithmetic.

Gilbert, sweetest uncle,
saddest vato on the block,
moved back in with his parents
the summer he wasn't locked up.
His P.O. warned it was the worst
place to stay clean.

I remember the night, loaded
on whiskey & H, he played guitar

while his mama
scorched the air in protest

howling in the wake of her son's
audible grief, the inconvenient
drawl of requiem.

Each song pulled from him
like something stolen,
he sang until the starless night
caved in on itself. Throat
a wounded calf limping
across the floorboards.

*Mama! mama! You never loved us,*
*did you? Mama, why didn't you try?*
he sang, in the greenest
voice ever invented.

She stood silent in the doorway
as he reached for her—
a child beckoned
by a cursed spindle
&
without offering the grace
of a single word
she turned her back to him,
strolled into the kitchen
& turned the radio on.

What name would you have chosen for yourself at birth if you got
to choose?

What stands out to you about the poem? What do you notice?

What role does silence play in this poem? What/who is silent, who/what
makes noise?

Who are the characters in this poem? What do we learn about each
of them?

What actions do each of the characters take, including the speaker?
What do you make of the differences between these actions?

What happens when the characters in the poem interact?

Who stays in this poem? Who leaves?

What is consumed in this poem?

How does this poem use and indicate time?

Which of the five senses would you say dominates this poem? Why?

How would it impact your reading of this poem if it were in present tense instead of past?

What images stand out to you in the poem? What do you picture when you close your eyes and think of this poem?

Read only the verbs in the poem. Does this illuminate anything about it to you?

*Read these instructions aloud to the workshop participants, giving them time to carry out each instruction before moving on to the next one.*

(1) Consider a time you found out or were told something you didn't want to know.

(2) With that memory in mind, write down a full sentence including whatever comes up for you as answers to the following questions:

- What animal were you when you discovered this thing?
  (Example: *I was an anteater when I discovered this thing.*)
- Where in your body did you feel that knowing?
- What animal was the information you received?
- Who could have warned you that this information/discovery was coming?
- Where did you put the information after you received it?
- What musical instrument did you become after you received this information?
- Who could play that musical instrument?

(3) Complete your worksheet.

(4) Pass the worksheet to the person on your right.

(5) Using the circled items as guidance, along with your answers to the questions, freewrite a poem describing that time you found out or were told something you didn't want to know.

Circle one of the two options in each row:

| | |
|---|---|
| Sing | Hush |
| Stay | Leave |
| Tragedy | Comedy |
| Star-filled | Starless |
| Radio | Guitar |
| Fall | Spring |

# WANTING A CHILD

## Marie Howe

I wanted to write about God and suffering and how the trees endure
    what we
don't want—the long dead months before the appalling blossoms.

But I think about James instead,
how last night, when he stood in the doorway bare-chested, I leaned
    down and

pressed my cheek against his belly,
and drew the side of my face up over his chest, his shoulder and throat

and chin and cheek. I did it over and over again,
leaning down and dragging my cheek up against him.

Tonight Jane sleeps between white hospital sheets. She's already lost
    her hair
from treatment. Two more years of it: six months on, six months off,

I almost envy the simplicity of her life,
deprived of a certain future.

Snowy evening in a dark snowy winter:
daffodils in a glass vase on the mantel over the fireplace that doesn't work.

The radiator's squeak and whine.
Plows soon, their deep and decent rumbling. Then more night,

more snow and wind, and in the morning, somebody shoveling.

When was the last time you remember feeling envious?

## DISCUSSION QUESTIONS

What stands out to you about the poem? What do you notice?

What sound do you hear repeating in the beginning portion of the poem? How does that affect your reading of it?

What accumulates in this poem?

Who is named in the poem? What do we learn about them?

What desires are named in the poem?

What is the role of inanimate objects in the poem? Are there any places in this poem where objects stand in for feelings?

How does the poet use sentence structure—complete sentences, fragments, the piling up of clauses, etc.?

Which of the five senses dominates this poem?

If you close your eyes and picture this poem, what color do you see?

How would you describe the tone of the beginning of the poem? How does that change through the poem, if it does? How would you describe the tone or feeling at the end of the poem?

What is happening right now in the poem? What happened in the past? What is predicted to happen in the future?

How does the order in which information is presented in this poem affect your reading of it? How would the poem be different if the stanzas were arranged in a different order?

## Exercise

*Read these instructions aloud to the workshop participants, giving them time to carry out each instruction before moving on to the next one.*

Make a note of each of these things as I read them out. Don't worry about being right or making sense—just write whatever comes to mind.

Write down:

- Something you want quite badly.
- Something you've wanted to write about but not been able to.
- A plant or object that reminds you of that thing you've wanted to write about.
- A person you've interacted with recently.
- Two actions or gestures you've made while interacting with that person.
- Someone you love who is far away.
- One characteristic of that person who is far away.
- Something you love or envy about that person.
- Five words to describe what's happening outside right now.
- Five words to describe what's happening around you right now.
- Five words to describe what will happen tomorrow.

Title the poem based on the thing that you want. Use the rest of your list as the basis for your freewrite, going in any order you like. If you feel stuck on getting started, begin with "I wanted to write about..."

# PRAYER OF THE BACKHANDED

## *Jericho Brown*

Not the palm, not the pear tree
Switch, not the broomstick,
Nor the closest extension
Cord, not his braided belt, but God,
Bless the back of my daddy's hand
Which, holding nothing tightly
Against me and not wrapped
In leather, eliminated the air
Between itself and my cheek.
Make full this dimpled cheek
Unworthy of its unfisted print
And forgive my forgetting
The love of a hand
Hungry for reflex, a hand that took
No thought of its target
Like hail from a blind sky,
Involuntary, fast, but brutal
In its bruising. Father, I bear the bridge
Of what might have been
A broken nose. I lift to you
What was a busted lip. Bless
The boy who believes
His best beatings lack
Intention, the mark of the beast.
Bring back to life the son
Who glories in the sin
Of immediacy, calling it love.
God, save the man whose arm

Like an angel's invisible wing
May fly backward in fury
Whether or not his son stands near.
Help me hold in place my blazing jaw
As I think to say excuse me.

What's the last rule you broke?

What stands out to you about the poem? What do you notice?

With what does the poem begin? How do we start, and how does this ready you for the poem?

To whom is the poem addressed?

Who are the characters in the poem?

What things are asked of God in this poem?
- *Bless the back of my daddy's hand*
- *forgive my forgetting / The love of a hand / Hungry for reflex*
- *Bless / The boy who believes / His best beatings lack / Intention*
- *Bring back to life the son / Who glories in the sin / Of immediacy, calling it love*
- *God, save the man whose arm / Like an angel's invisible wing / May fly backward in fury*
- *Help me hold in place my blazing jaw*

Look at the line breaks—which lines, if any, stand out as having meanings independent of the lines around them/their containing sentence? (For example: "the boy who believes," "of what might have been," etc.)

What changes, if any, do you notice in terms of sentence length and structure as the poem proceeds? How does this impact you as a reader/ listener?

What role does intention play in this poem? Who does or does not exhibit intention, and to what end?

What words for a male parent are used in the poem? To whom or to what do they refer?

How is sound used in this poem? Are there places where the sound stands out, either supporting or contradicting the meaning of the words or line?

Read just the last word of each line. Does this illuminate anything about the poem?

*Before the workshop, cut enough slips of paper for each participant to have five. Put out one bowl large enough to contain them all.*

*Read these instructions aloud to the workshop participants, giving them time to carry out each instruction before moving on to the next one.*

(1) You each have five slips of paper. On each one, write down a specific authority figure, real or imaginary/fictional. For example, the chief of police, God, Grandma Julie, etc.

Put all five slips of paper in the bowl. Once everyone has placed their papers in the bowl, pass it around. Each choose five slips—it's fine if you get your own.

(2) In Christian theology, there are seven deadly sins: gluttony, sloth, greed, lust, jealousy, wrath, and pride.

What are your seven deadly sins? These can be serious, lighthearted, or a mixture.

For example:
- *the sin of procrastination*
- *the sin of impossible expectations*
- *the sin of perfectionism*
- *the sin of double standards*
- *the sin of dissatisfaction*
- *the sin of shifted blame*
- *the sin of condescension*

Choose one of those and circle it.

(3) Think of a time you committed the sin you circled.

(4) Choose one of the authority figures you pulled from the bowl. Freewrite a poem asking them to either punish or forgive you for committing this sin.

# LOOSE STRIFE

*Quan Barry*


Somebody says draw a map. Populate it with the incidents
of your childhood. Mark the spot where the lake receded
after a winter of light snow. The stairs on which someone
slapped you. The place where the family dog hung itself
by jumping over the back fence while still on the dog run,
hours later its body like a limp flag on a windless day.
Draw a map, someone says. Let yourself remember.
In the refugee camp a hundred thousand strong
draw the stony outcrop from which you could no longer see
the plume of smoke that was your village. Draw a square
for the bathroom stall where Grandpa hid each day
in order to eat his one egg free from the starving eyes
of his classmates, an X for the courthouse where you and he
were naturalized, a broken line for the journey. Draw a map,
Jon says. Let it be your way into the poem. Here is where
that plane filled with babies crashed that I was not on.
Here is where I was ashamed. On the second floor
at Pranash University the people wait their turn. Have you
drawn your map, Jon asks. He has rolled up his sleeves.
Forty-five minutes to noon the Prince stands up and says
that the monks must be excused. We watch them file out,
saffron robes as if their bodies have burst into blossom.
Draw a map. Fly halfway around the globe. Here is the room
next to the library where you realize how poor your tradition is,
the local people with poetic forms still in use that date back
to the time of Christ. Tell us about your map. Explain
how these wavy lines represent the river, this rectangle
the school-turned-prison where only seven

escaped with their lives. This is my map. This star the place
where I sat in a roomful of people among whom not one
was not touched by genocide. Every last map resplendent with death
though nobody knows where their loved ones lie buried.
How many times can I appropriate a story that is not mine to tell?
The woman stands up and says she is not a poet, that she
doesn't have the words. She points to a triangle on a piece of paper.
Here is the spot where she found human bones in the well
of her childhood home, and how her mother told her
*don't be afraid* because it was not the work of wild animals.

What irrational fear do you possess that you're willing to share with the group?

What stands out to you about the poem? What do you notice?

What visual images stand out to you in the poem?

Where does the "I" enter the poem? When does it come back? How does this affect your reading of the poem?

Who are the characters in the poem?

Who is named in the poem? What happens once "Jon" is named?

What is the role of metaphor (a thing representing another thing) in the poem?

What is the structural organizing principle of the poem? Is there more than one? Which is central?

If we look at the word "map" as marking sections of the poem, what does that do to your understanding of it?

What words/concepts aside from the map are repeated in the poem? To what effect?

What do you make of the title? How would it be different if the title included a reference to map, geography, etc.?

List all of the command words (i.e., "draw") in the poem. What, if anything, does this illuminate?

Read the first two words of each sentence in the poem. What, if anything, does this illuminate?

*Read these instructions aloud to the workshop participants, giving them time to carry out each instruction before moving on to the next one.*

(1) Write down a series of at least 10 command/instruction words (draw, dance, lose, bomb, forget, etc.).

(2) Make a list of at least 10 physical objects.

(3) Link each command/instruction with one of the objects using "a" or "an." Example: draw a map, dance an apple, bomb a lilac tree, etc.

(4) Choose one of those phrases as your "command phrase."

(5) Start the poem with "Someone says _____ (command phrase)." Example: *Someone says bomb a lilac tree.*

(6) Repeat the command phrase at irregular intervals throughout the poem.

# INVENTORY

## *Joan Larkin*

One who lifted his arms with joy, first time across the finish line
    at the New York marathon, six months later a skeleton
    falling from threshold to threshold, shit streaming from
    his diaper,
one who walked with a stick, wore a well-cut suit to the opera,
    to poetry readings, to mass, who wrote the best long poem
    of his life at Roosevelt Hospital and read it on television,
one who went to 35 funerals in 12 months,
one who said *I'm sick of all you AIDS widows,*
one who lost both her sisters,
one who said *I'm not sure that what he and I do is safe, but we're*
    *young, I don't think we'll get sick,*
one who dying said *They came for me in their boat, they want me*
    *on it, and I told them Not tonight, I'm staying here with James,*
one who went to Mexico for Laetrile,
one who went to California for Compound Q,
one who went to Germany for extract of Venus' flytrap,
one who went to France for humane treatment,
one who chanted, holding hands in a circle,
one who ate vegetables, who looked in a mirror and said
    *I forgive you.*
one who refused to see his mother,
one who refused to speak to his brother,
one who refused to let a priest enter his room,
one who did the best paintings of his life and went home from
    his opening in a taxi with twenty kinds of flowers,
one who moved to San Francisco and lived two more years,
one who married his lover and died next day,

one who said *I'm entirely filled with anger*,

one who said *I don't have AIDS, I have something else*,

one with night sweats, nausea, fever, who worked as a nurse,

one who kept on studying to be a priest,

one who kept on photographing famous women,

one who kept on writing vicious reviews,

one who kept going to AA meetings till he couldn't walk,

one whose son came just once to the hospital,

one whose mother said *This is God's judgment*,

one whose father held him when he was frightened,

one whose minister said *Beth and her lover of twelve years were devoted as Ruth and Naomi*,

one whose clothes were thrown in the street, beautiful shirts and ties a neighbor picked from the garbage and handed out at a party,

one who said *This room is a fucking prison*,

one who said *They're so nice to me here*,

one who cut my hair and said *My legs bother me*,

one who couldn't stand, who said *I like those earrings*,

one with a tube in his chest, who asked *What are you eating?*

one who said *How's your writing? Are you moving to the mountains?* who said *I hope you get rich*,

one who said *Death is transition*,

one who was doing new work, entirely filled with anger,

one who wanted to live till his birthday, and did.

What is something someone said to you once that you'll never forget?

What stands out to you about the poem? What do you notice?

How does the title influence your reading of the poem?

Does your understanding of the title change once you've read the whole poem?

How does the use of "one who" impact you as a reader? How would the poem feel different if it used names or pronouns like he, she, or they?

Who or what gets named in this poem?

How does the use of past tense affect you as a reader or listener?

How does the poet balance detail and generality in the poem?

Does the speaker ever appear in the poem? How does that appearance or non-appearance affect your experience of the poem?

Aside from "one who," what words or phrases repeat in the poem? What is the impact of this repetition?

What is the role of geography in this poem?

In what ways does this poem establish, use, and/or subvert expectations on the part of the reader or listener?

*Before the workshop, print out copies of the worksheet for all participants to use in the exercise.*

*Read these instructions aloud to the workshop participants, giving them time to carry out each instruction before moving on to the next one.*

(1) Consider something that affects many people you know, as well as people you don't. For example, cancer, the threat of police violence, relentless optimism, etc. Make a note of this.

(2) Brainstorm a list of at least 12 people you know, or know of, directly or indirectly affected by this thing.

(3) Look at that list and for each person, write down something they did, said, and/or experienced.

(4) Decide whether you want your litany to use "one," "he/she/they," "you," or the name + *who*.

(5) Draw from your list and freewrite a litany using that starter ("One who" or "She who" or "You who" or "<name> who"). Feel free to add people or details or to break the form entirely.

Worksheet

Thing: _____

| NAME | DETAIL |
|------|--------|
|  |  |
|  |  |
|  |  |
|  |  |
|  |  |
|  |  |
|  |  |
|  |  |
|  |  |
|  |  |
|  |  |
|  |  |
|  |  |

# WHAT IT LOOK LIKE

## *Terrance Hayes*

Dear Ol' Dirty Bastard: I too like it raw,
I don't especially care for Duke Ellington
at a birthday party. I care less and less
about the shapes of shapes because forms
change and nothing is more durable than feeling.
My uncle used the money I gave him
to buy a few vials of what looked like candy
after the party where my grandma sang
in an outfit that was obviously made
for a West African king. My motto is
*Never mistake what it is for what it looks like.*
My generosity, for example, is mostly a form
of vanity. A bandanna is a useful handkerchief,
but a handkerchief is a useless-ass bandanna.
This only looks like a footnote in my report
concerning the party. *Trill* stands for what is
*truly real* though it may be hidden by the houses
just over the hills between us, by the hands
on the bars between us. That picture
of my grandmother with my uncle
when he was a baby is not trill. What it is
is the feeling felt seeing garbagemen drift
along the predawn avenues, a sloppy slow rain
taking its time to the coast. Milquetoast
is not trill, nor is bouillabaisse. *Bakku-shan*
is Japanese for a woman who is beautiful
only when viewed from behind. Like I was saying,
my motto is *Never mistake what it looks like*

*for what it is* else you end up like that Negro
Othello. (Was Othello a Negro?) Don't you lie
about who you are sometimes and then realize
the lie is true? You are blind to your power, Brother
Bastard, like the king who wanders his kingdom
searching for the king. And that's okay.
No one will tell you you are the king.
No one really wants a king anyway.

What musician or other celebrity do you feel you'd be friends with if you ever met?

DISCUSSION QUESTIONS

What stands out to you about the poem? What do you notice?

How does the title bring you into the poem? What kind of expectations does it set?

To whom is the poem directed? How does this influence your reading of it?

How does the writer investigate the nature of language, of words themselves, in this poem?

What gets defined in this poem, and how?

Who gets named in this poem?

How does this poem investigate what *seems* versus what *is*?

If you were making a film of this poem, what are some of the camera directions you'd provide? (For example, zoom in here, or pan out there, close-up, etc.)

Read just the first two words of each sentence in the poem. Does this illuminate or change anything about your understanding of the poem?

How does the writer use enjambment—breaking sentences across lines or stanzas—in this poem?

How does the speaker in this poem establish their authority?

Where do you see contradiction used in this poem? How does that affect you as a reader?

What is repeated in the poem? What is the effect of this repetition?

How would you describe the tone of this poem at the beginning? At the end?

# Exercise

*Read these instructions aloud to the workshop participants, giving them time to carry out each instruction before moving on to the next one.*

(1) Choose a musician or other celebrity with whom you feel a particular connection.

(2) I'm going to give you a series of instructions. For each, just freewrite whatever comes to mind until I give the next prompt.

Try to keep writing without stopping—push yourself to keep the pen or typing fingers moving, even if what you're writing is nonsense or about the fact that you have no idea what to write.

- Write down Dear _____, filling in the name of your celebrity friend.
- Write a sentence starting with "I too" that lets them know what you have in common.
- Write a sentence about something you don't care about.
- Tell a story involving a family member.
- Describe something someone was wearing in that story.
- What is your motto? Write it down.
  (Remember not to overthink this—it doesn't have to be your "real" motto.)
- Tell about a time when you lived out that motto, or confess to never living it out.
- Talk more about that thing you have in common with your celebrity.
- Describe a real or invented family photo.

- Say something about the weather.
- Give us another version of your motto.
- Tell your celebrity something they don't know.

# INVENTION

## *Tina Chang*

On an island, an open road
where an animal has been crushed
by something larger than itself.

It is mangled by four o'clock light, soul
sour-sweet, intestines flattened and raked
by the sun, eyes still savage.

This landscape of Taiwan looks like a body
black and blue. On its coastline mussels have cracked
their faces on rocks, clouds collapse

onto tiny houses, and just now a monsoon has begun.
It reminds me of a story my father told me:
He once made the earth not in seven days

but in one. His steely joints wielded lava and water
and mercy in great ionic perfection.
He began the world, hammering the length

of trees, trees like a war of families,
trees which fumbled for grand gesture.
The world began in an explosion of fever and rain.

He said, *Tina, your body came out floating.*
I was born in the middle of monsoon season,
palm trees tearing the tin roofs.

Now as I wander to the center of the island
no one will speak to me. My dialect left somewhere
in his pocket, in a nursery book,

a language of child's play. Everything unfurls
in pictures: soil is washed from the soles of feet, a woman
runs toward her weeping son, chicken bones float

in a pot full of dirty water.
I return to the animal on the road.
When I stoop to look at it,

smells of trash, rotting vegetation,
the pitiful tongue, claws curled tight
to its heart; eyes open, eyes open.

When the world began in the small factory
of my father's imagination, he never spoke
of this gnarled concoction of bone and blood

that is nothing like wonder but just the opposite,
something simply ravaged. He would die soon
after the making of the world. I would go on waking,

sexing, mimicking enemies. I would go on coaxed
by gravity and hard science. While he rested in the satin
of his shriveled skin. Eyes swollen to exquisite planets.

What is the farthest you've ever traveled?

## DISCUSSION QUESTIONS

What stands out to you about the poem? What do you notice?

Where does the poem begin?

How is the body used in the poem?

What is the role of time in the poem? What happens in the past, and what happens now and in the future?

What cycles do you see occurring and recurring in the poem?

What is the role of spoken language in the poem?

When you close your eyes after hearing or reading the poem, what do you see?

How does the writer's use of enjambment—breaking sentences across lines and stanzas—affect your reading of the poem? Are there any sentences that are not enjambed? What is the impact of that?

Read just the last word of each line. Does this reveal anything about the poem?

Read just the verbs in the poem. Does this reveal anything about the poem?

# Exercise

*Before the workshop, print out copies of the worksheet for all participants to use in the exercise.*

*Read these instructions aloud to the workshop participants, giving them time to carry out each instruction before moving on to the next one.*

(1) List in the first column:
- A place you have visited
- A family member
- A body part
- A kind of fabric
- A verb
- A verb
- A verb

(2) In the second column, list the opposite of each. Don't worry about making sense! The opposite of Disney World might be your basement, or the public library, or the dentist.

(3) In the third column, list an opposite of the word in the second column. Don't go back to the first column's word—get creative!

(4) Begin your freewrite in the location from the third column, starting with "on" or "in" or "at." For example, "At Disney World's Haunted Castle…"

At some point in the poem, introduce the family member, body part, and fabric from any column. Use any of the verbs as well.

|  |  |  |
|---|---|---|
|  |  |  |
|  |  |  |
|  |  |  |
|  |  |  |
|  |  |  |
|  |  |  |

# SHALL WE DANCE

*FOR MP*

## Patrick Rosal

This is for you, asleep, right now, curled up
in your big bed, alone, turned
away from the window facing the river,
the taste of Spanish wine maybe
somewhere in your mouth, you,
who might never dream of bluefish scales
or apricots knocked about in buckets
or shiny pianos locked away
in bright lit rooms. Wait.
Let me slow down, pause
a moment before I wish
one good reckless kiss toward
you who won't wake for a few hours
more, rise, dress, and ride the dark
headed to no work you love.

Knowing how much you can't stand
this city when it rains,
let me send you this first: a small
torrent by surprise one night
as you stand in flip flops on some curb
in Chinatown, drenched, your favorite
outfit slightly ruined and you,
with your hands thrown up
in disgust, laughing your ass off. I say,
tomorrow let's drink no wine, but dance
on one of those west side piers.

And like that one summer night
the dock swayed beneath us
and you clapped so hard
you busted your watch
and bruised your palms,
let the beats be free and deep.
Let the air be cold. Let me, finally,
deliver to you three syllables
that sound like the name of someone
you can't bring yourself to love so easily,
three small stones that, together, will
make no sense, but will linger
in the world you dream, a place
where similar things rarely converge,
where, rather, they whisper
to each other across entire seas.

Let there never be entire seas
between you and me
for long. And if it must be
that way, if some god decides
to lay down between me and you
one hundred submerged
provinces, let me seek out the closest
shore one cold morning, looking out
from my own nation toward
the nation you are sleeping in
and listen, above the blare of the surf
trashing its million chandeliers,
for something slight, and not quite
lost, like the sound of your sleeves
passing across your wrists.

What is your favorite memory of rain?

What stands out to you about the poem? What do you notice?

What do we learn about the "you" in the poem? What do we learn about the speaker, and the relationship between them?

How does the poet use sentence structure—length, clauses, variation—in this poem?

Where and how does the poet use enjambment (continuing a sentence across a line break or stanza)? How does that impact your reading of the poem?

Does one of the five senses dominate this poem? If so, which one?

What details stand out to you in the poem?

What moves in the poem? What remains still?

What would you say is the central feeling of this poem?

In what ways do the sounds in the poem reflect or create tension with its content?

If you had to choose one line or sentence as the heart of the poem, which would it be?

# Exercise

*Read these instructions aloud to the workshop participants, giving them time to carry out each instruction before moving on to the next one.*

(1) Thinking about that favorite memory of rain you shared, write down one complete sentence—anything you like. Make sure the people sitting on either side of you can't see what you write.

(2) Remember the game of "telephone" you may have played as a kid? We're going to do that now with our sentences.

Whisper what you wrote to the person to your right, then listen to the person to your left. Repeat the sentence you just heard—without checking to make sure you have it correct—to the person on your right. Repeat until you hear your own sentence (or some variation thereof) back.

Write this sentence down, whether it has changed or not.

(3) Decide who you want to direct your poem to—choose someone involved in that memory or to whom you want to describe the memory.

(4) List (or invent) seven characteristics of that person:

- Where do they sleep?
- What is one article of jewelry they are wearing?
- What is the last thing they drank?
- What do they think of the rain?
- What sound do they love?
- What do they dream about?

(5) Freewrite starting with the sentence you whispered, and ending with the sentence that came back to you—might be the same sentence, slightly changed, or very different.

The Gathering Voices approach is intended to provide a platform for community-based work in a broad range of settings. The poems, discussion questions, and writing prompts included in each workshop are geared toward an adult community group, but both the approach and the workshop materials can be adapted for use in classrooms and academic settings as well.

Following are some ideas and insights as to how this book can be used in these more structured environments, and/or with younger workshop participants.

The fundamental premise of the Gathering Voices workshop is that poems are made things, and can therefore be read and discussed by almost anyone. Beginning with this sense of possibility and starting with the obvious—"what do you notice about this poem"—can open the door to discussion even among students who may believe themselves unprepared to analyze poems.

Likewise, many of the discussion questions can serve as conversation prompts for full classrooms of students or for small breakout groups. For example, after hearing and reading the poem "Alabanza" by Martín Espada, a class could break out into small groups, each assigned a different question/aspect of the poem to discuss:

- *Sound*: How is sound used in the poem—both the sounds of words and what is heard or spoken?
- *Cast of characters*: Who are the characters in this poem? What do we learn about each of them?

- *Place*: What is the role of geographic location in the poem? Where do we begin, where do we go, where do we end?
- *Repetition*: What words and concepts repeat in this poem? What is the impact of this repetition?
- *Structure and pattern*: What pattern is established in the poem's structure? Where does this pattern change? Does this reflect a change in content or perspective as well?

Alternatively, the writing prompts can, in most cases, be extracted and used to stimulate writing among students without a discussion of the poem included in the full workshop description. As another option, while many of these poems contain language that might preclude their use in a traditional classroom setting, other poems by these same writers may be found and combined with the writing prompts.

Also of note is that all of the poems included in this book were written by poets who are alive and writing today. As a result, many of these poems or others by these same poets can be found online in audio and video, and streamed for classroom use. Hearing the poem in the voice of the poet can be a powerful tool for introducing students to the kind of work included in this book.

*This is sample text—adapt it to suit your own style and tone!*

Hello wonderfuls! This is your confirmation for Friday's workshop to be held at 2601 W. Main Street, first floor.

Important info:

- Please plan to arrive between 7 and 7:25 p.m., so that we can start promptly at 7:30. We will end by about 10 p.m.
- If circumstances change and you won't be able to attend, please call or text 555-555-1234 ASAP.
- The workshop will involve discussion of the attached poem, as well as group critique of three poems from participants drawn randomly from a hat, and a freewrite period using a prompt drawn from the poem.
- If you plan to put your name in the hat, please bring 10 copies of your poem.
- Please bring something to write on or with—pen and paper, laptop, etc.
- There is no set price for the workshop, but a hat is passed for the suggested $10 donation. No one will be turned away for lack of funds.
- Feel free to bring beverages and snacks to partake of and share!

As always, the workshop practices and commitments are attached—feel free to reach out with any questions or concerns.

Marty

Welcome to the Gathering Voices workshop! These are the basic principles and practices we use to guide our time together. By joining the workshop, you agree to abide by these and to actively support the maintenance of a positive, challenging Gathering Voices community.

If you have any questions or concerns, feel free to reach out to me at samplemail@mailserver.com or 555-555-1234.

Fundamental practices:

- *Curiosity* about new perspectives, approaches, and possibilities, as opposed to criticism and competition.
- *Receptivity* to ideas, to art, to each other.
- *Joy* in the work and in the community.
- *Rigor* in our approach to growth, both our own and other people's.

Commitments:

- We value the potential, the experience, and the perspective each person brings. This is reflected in our words, actions, and attitudes.
- We approach poems not as broken things in need of fixing, nor as objects of like or dislike, but as subjects of study and analysis, artworks whose possibilities we get to unpack.
- We come ready to work. Eager to engage. Committed to creating a positive, challenging environment for everyone.

**MARTY MCCONNELL** is the winner of the 2017 Michael Waters Poetry Prize for her forthcoming second poetry collection *when they say you can't go home again, what they mean is you were never there* and the author of *Gathering Voices: Creating a Community-Based Poetry Workshop*, published by YesYes Books. Her first full-length collection, *wine for a shotgun*, published by EM Press, received the Silver Medal in the Independent Publishers Awards, and was a finalist for both the Audre Lorde Award (Publishing Triangle) and the Lambda Literary Awards. McConnell transplanted herself from Chicago to New York City in 1999, after completing the first of three national tours with The Morrigan, an all-female performance poetry troupe she co-founded. She received her MFA in creative writing/poetry from Sarah Lawrence College, and for nearly a decade, co-curated the flagship reading series of the New York City-based louderARTS Project. She returned to Chicago in 2009 to launch Vox Ferus, an organization dedicated to empowering and energizing individuals and communities through the written and spoken word.

ALSO FROM YESYES BOOKS

**Full-Length Collections**

*i be, but i ain't* by Aziza Barnes

*The Feeder* by Jennifer Jackson Berry

*Gutter* by Lauren Brazeal

*What Runs Over* by Kayleb Rae Candrilli

*Love the Stranger* by Jay Deshpande

*Blues Triumphant* by Jonterri Gadson

*North of Order* by Nicholas Gulig

*Meet Me Here at Dawn* by Sophie Klahr

*I Don't Mind If You're Feeling Alone* by Thomas Patrick Levy

*Sons of Achilles* by Nabila Lovelace

*Reaper's Milonga* by Lucian Mattison

*If I Should Say I Have Hope* by Lynn Melnick

*Landscape with Sex and Violence* by Lynn Melnick

*GOOD MORNING AMERICA I AM HUNGRY AND ON FIRE*
   by jamie mortara

*some planet* by jamie mortara

*Boyishly* by Tanya Olson

*A Falling Knife Has No Handle* by Emily O'Neill

*Pelican* by Emily O'Neill

*The Youngest Butcher in Illinois* by Robert Ostrom

*A New Language for Falling Out of Love* by Meghan Privitello

*I'm So Fine: A List of Famous Men & What I Had On* by Khadijah Queen

*American Barricade* by Danniel Schoonebeek

*The Anatomist* by Taryn Schwilling

*Gilt* by Raena Shirali

*Panic Attack, USA* by Nate Slawson

*[insert] boy* by Danez Smith

*Man vs Sky* by Corey Zeller

*The Bones of Us* by J. Bradley
   [ Art by Adam Scott Mazer ]

## Chapbook Collections

**VINYL 45S**

*After* by Fatimah Asghar

*Inside My Electric City* by Caylin Capra-Thomas

*Dream with a Glass Chamber* by Aricka Foreman

*Pepper Girl* by Jonterri Gadson

*Of Darkness and Tumbling* by Mónica Gomery

*Bad Star* by Rebecca Hazelton

*Makeshift Cathedral* by Peter LaBerge

*Still, the Shore* by Keith Leonard

*Please Don't Leave Me Scarlett Johansson* by Thomas Patrick Levy

*Juned* by Jenn Marie Nunes

*A History of Flamboyance* by Justin Phillip Reed

*No* by Ocean Vuong

*This American Ghost* by Michael Wasson


**BLUE NOTE EDITIONS**

*Beastgirl & Other Origin Myths* by Elizabeth Acevedo

*Kissing Caskets* by Mahogany L. Browne

*One Above One Below: Positions & Lamentations*
by Gala Mukomolova


**COMPANION SERIES**

*Inadequate Grave* by Brandon Courtney

*The Rest of the Body* by Jay Deshpande